Following Faith with P. T. Forsyth

Peter Taylor Forsyth

Following Faith with P. T. Forsyth

DAILY DEVOTIONS

Donald K. McKim

CASCADE *Books* • Eugene, Oregon

FOLLOWING FAITH WITH P. T. FORSYTH
Daily Devotions

Copyright © 2022 Donald K. McKim. All rights reserved. Except for brief quotations in critical publications or reviews, no part of this book may be reproduced in any manner without prior written permission from the publisher. Write: Permissions, Wipf and Stock Publishers, 199 W. 8th Ave., Suite 3, Eugene, OR 97401.

Cascade Books
An Imprint of Wipf and Stock Publishers
199 W. 8th Ave., Suite 3
Eugene, OR 97401

www.wipfandstock.com

PAPERBACK ISBN: 978-1-6667-1736-5
HARDCOVER ISBN: 978-1-6667-1737-2
EBOOK ISBN: 978-1-6667-1738-9

Cataloguing-in-Publication data:

Names: McKim, Donald K. [author].

Title: Following faith with P. T. Forsyth : daily devotions / Donald K. McKim.

Description: Eugene, OR: Cascade Books, 2022 | Includes bibliographic references

Identifiers: ISBN 978-1-6667-1736-5 (paperback) | ISBN 978-1-6667-1737-2 (hardcover) | ISBN 978-1-6667-1738-9 (ebook)

Subjects: LCSH: Forsyth, Peter Taylor, 1848–1921 | Spiritual life | Religious life | Theology, Doctrinal | Pastoral theology

Classification: BX7260.F583 M35 2022 (print) | BX7260.F583 (ebook)

*For LindaJo and
for our family:
Stephen and Caroline, Maddie, Annie, Jack, and Ford,
and Karl and Lauren.
In thanksgiving to God!*

Contents

Preface xi
Introduction xv
Using This Book xviii

BELIEVING AS A CHRISTIAN

1. The Word of God Is the Gospel 3
2. Christ Came to Bring a Gospel 5
3. God's Initiative of Free Grace 7
4. God Gave Us Himself 9
5. A Trinitarian God 11
6. A Gracious God 13
7. God is Holy Love 15
8. Sin Is Utterly Irrational 17
9. Sin Is Not Our Life-Principle 19
10. Christ Came to Effect Forgiveness 21
11. The Kingdom Breaking In 23
12. What Is Faith? 25
13. The Work of the Holy Spirit 27
14. The Spirit Brings Regeneration 29
15. Christ Was Born to Die 31
16. What Love! 33

Contents

17. Atonement Makes Repentance 35
18. Kingdom—Act and Gift of God 37
19. From Hostility to Peace 39
20. Judgment Comes Down in Mercy 41
21. Atonement Flowed from Grace 43
22. Speaking Faith 45
23. God's Message Is God's Own Self 47
24. Faith *Is* Salvation 49
25. The Church's One Foundation 51
26. One Church in Various Places 53
27. Enter Christ, Enter the Church 55
28. Pardon Is New Birth 57
29. Love Is Faith in Its Perfect Form 59
30. Begin with the Grace of God 61
31. Ministry as Evangelical Succession 63
32. A God Who Knows Us 65
33. Living Hope from Christ's Resurrection 67
34. A Sacrament Does Something 69
35. The Purpose of the World 71
36. The Greatest Function of the Church 73
37. In Christ Jesus by Faith 75
38. Finished Reconciliation 77
39. Christ Redeemed the Human Race 79
40. Christ Is Savior of the World 81
41. God's Holy Love Is Omnipotent Forever 83
42. Heaven Laughs Last 85

CONTENTS

LIVING AS A CHRISTIAN

43. The Organized Hallelujah 89
44. Daily Cleansings of Channels of Grace 91
45. The Greatest Benefit in Life 93
46. Trust the Bad to the Merciful God 95
47. A Living Piety 97
48. Where Is Your Heart? 99
49. Faith and Praise 101
50. Believe, Be, and Abide in Christ 103
51. Living Communion 105
52. A Personal Christ 107
53. On Eternal Rock 109
54. Saints 111
55. Holy People Don't Feel They are Holy 113
56. Sin Which Stays and Sin Which Visits 115
57. Speaking with God 117
58. We Live . . . to Pray 119
59. The Highest Dependence on God 121
60. Ask for Everything in Christ's Name 123
61. Obedient Acceptance 125
62. Final Forgiveness in Christ 127
63. Christ Intercedes for Us 129
64. Ministry of the Word 131
65. The Kingdom in the Making 133
66. The Counterpart of Christ 135
67. Prayer Is Asking and Action 137
68. Trusting What Christ Did 139

Contents

69. Become What We Are and Are Not 141
70. God's Desire Is Communion with Us 143
71. Forgiveness of Old Life and New 145
72. A New Heart 147
73. All the Accounts Are Kept 149
74. Concrete Prayer 151
75. Our Chief Certainty 153
76. Faith Is Obedience 155
77. God Is for Us 157
78. Faith as Personal Trust 159
79. Sacraments as the Word Visible 161
80. Relation to God over Behavior 163
81. Church Is New Creation of God in the Holy Spirit 165
82. Adjusting the Compass 167
83. The Condensation of History 169
84. All Is Well 171

Sources Cited 173
Selected Resources for Further Reflection 175
Electronic Resources 177

Preface

I have long been interested in Peter Taylor (P. T.) Forsyth (1848–1921).

Throughout my theological studies, Forsyth's name has been a companion in various ways. His books have been informative and formative for me. His emphases have been salutary for my theological understandings and also for my personal faith.

Both these elements combine in *Following Faith with P. T. Forsyth: Daily Devotions*. This book is one of a number I have written to be a "theological devotional" book that introduces important theologians by presenting a short quotation followed by my discussion of the quotation's theological meaning combined with comments about the importance of this insight for Christian life today. My hope is to provide accessible devotional readings that will help inform our Christian faith and our Christian lives.

Forsyth's writings are particularly open to this approach. Forsyth wrote bluntly and always with an eye toward the theological importance of what he had to say for the everyday lives of Christians. My hope is to convey Forsyth's theological directness with helpful insights into ways in which theological understandings can shape and inform who we are as Christians and ways our Christian experience can be deepened and become more vital.

I have been blessed by teachers and friends who have enhanced my interest in P. T. Forsyth. When I was a student at Pittsburgh Theological Seminary I studied with the incomparable Ford Lewis Battles, who admired Forsyth.

Preface

My teacher and later my doctoral supervisor, Robert S. Paul, a British Congregationalist who grew up in Forsyth's home church, had a strong interest in Forsyth, especially in his views of authority, atonement, and the church. In January 1973, I did an Independent Study with Dr. Paul on "The Authority of Scripture in P. T. Forsyth." This was most helpful since it immersed me in Forsyth's writings and especially on an important theological topic.

This work became part of the book I wrote with Jack B. Rogers, my former professor at Westminster College: *The Authority and Interpretation of the Bible: An Historical Approach* (1979). We saw P. T. Forsyth as one who reacted against the approach to the Bible taught by Reformed Scholasticism, which insisted on biblical inerrancy. In this, Rogers and I agreed, Forsyth was more in line with the sixteenth-century Protestant reformers.

A friend who was a scholar of Forsyth was Alan P. F. Sell. He, too, was a British Congregationalist who wrote widely and wisely and most often brought Forsyth into his work as a dialogue partner and exemplary theologian. Alan was editor and a contributor to *P. T. Forsyth: Prophet for a New Millennium*, published by The United Reformed Church (2000). His essay for the volume was the same as the book's title. I have quoted a bit of his conclusion in the Introduction that follows here.

A seminary friend who has gone on to contribute to Forsyth studies is Robert Benedetto. Bob was asked by Dikran Y. Hadidian, the Director of Barbour Library at Pittsburgh Seminary while we were students, to prepare a bibliography for a new edition of Forsyth's *Positive Preaching and Modern Mind* (1981). As a seminary librarian, Bob went on to incorporate this bibliographic work into his *P. T. Forsyth Bibliography and Index* (1993), which is indispensable for Forsyth studies. While I was writing this book, Bob sent along an unpublished manuscript of his on Forsyth which was very helpful to me. I am most grateful to Bob and for our friendship.

This book is dedicated to my family. I have dedicated books to each family member through the years. This one is dedicated to us all, together. My wife, LindaJo, is my dearest companion and light and love of my life. For our life together, through it all, I give her

Preface

deepest thanks and gratitude. Our sons and their families bring joys uncounted to our lives; and we delight in each of them: Stephen and Caroline and our grandchildren: Maddie, Annie, Jack, and Ford; and Karl and Lauren. We could not be more blessed than by the gift of our family love to share together. Thanks be to God!

Donald K. McKim
Germantown, Tennessee
Advent 2021

Introduction

P. T. FORSYTH (1848–1921) WAS a Scottish theologian, born in Aberdeen to humble parents. After serving twenty-five years in five pastorates in England as a Congregational pastor, Forsyth served for twenty years as principal of Hackney Congregational College, which became part of New College, London.[1]

Forsyth studied at the University of Aberdeen and then in Göttingen, under the liberal theologian Albrecht Ritschl (1822–89). But Forsyth came to reject liberal theology because he did not believe it accounted adequately for human sin and guilt. This led Forsyth to emphasize the atoning death and reconciliation of the world in Jesus Christ as the act of the God of holy love to provide forgiveness for the depths of human sin and a new life through faith in Jesus Christ. The victory of the cross of Christ in overcoming the cosmic tragedy of sin became Forsyth's way of interpreting the elements of Christian theology. His efforts were always directed toward proclaiming the Christian Gospel in his large number of books and articles as well as through preaching and speaking directly to the concerns of all people. His concern was to proclaim, as one interpreter put it: "The Christian message is not just an analysis of man's situation; it is the good news that

---

1. On Forsyth, see among other sources Donald G. Miller, "P. T. Forsyth: The Man" in Donald G. Miller, Browne Barr, and Robert S. Paul. *P. T. Forsyth: The Man, The Preachers' Theologian, Prophet for the 20th Century* including a reprint of P. T. Forsyth, *Positive Preaching and Modern Mind*. The Pittsburgh Theological Monograph Series, ed. Dikran Y. Hadidian, No. 36 (Pittsburgh: The Pickwick Press, 1981), 1–29.

Introduction

God has taken steps to meet and take care of that situation."[2] This reflects Forsyth's own testimony: "I was turned from a Christian to a believer, from a lover of love to an object of grace."[3] God's grace is given to the world fully and completely in the cross of Jesus Christ.

The enduring emphases of Forsyth's work have been recognized in various ways in the decades following his death. His works have been often reprinted and his "prophetic" voice has been called upon to speak important words for new eras to recapture the Gospel message. Thus Alan P. F. Sell wrote:

> Although our context is in many ways different from Forsyth's, we should do well to heed many reminders from him which tumble off his pages. Among these reminders are that God's love is holy love; that the Cross, understood as the fount of our salvation and the source of our new life, does and must hold central place; that fellowship in the Church is inescapable for Christians, because God calls a people for his praise and service; and that mission, conceived in the first place as a grateful response to God's unmerited grace, is an urgent matter.[4]

The devotions in this book seek to help us hear Forsyth's voice as he points us to Scripture and to the Gospel message to which Scripture testifies. The book is divided into two parts: "Believing as

---

2. Robert McAfee Brown, *P. T. Forsyth: Prophet for Today* (Philadelphia: The Westminster Press, 1952), 11.

3. P. T. Forsyth, *Positive Preaching and the Modern Mind*, The Lyman Beecher Lectures on Preaching, Yale University (London: Hodder & Stoughton, 1907), 282–83.

4. Alan P. F. Sell, "P. T. Forsyth Theologian for a New Millennium?" in Alan P. F. Sell, ed. *P. T. Forsyth: Prophet for a New Millennium?* (London: The United Reformed Church, 2000), 256. Put another way, Donald G. Miller wrote of Forsyth: "He was, as all are, a theologian of his time, yet was a theologian for all times, with insights that will abide the shifting impulses of the generations. He was, and will continue to be, a theologian who though at times bypassed and forgotten (because he tells us what we do not want to hear) will be rediscovered in the crises of life. His relevance, although superficially shaped in the thought struggles of his time, is timeless." See Donald G. Miller, "Foreword" in Robert Benedetto, *P. T. Forsyth Bibliography and Index*. Bibliographies and Indexes in Religious Studies, Number 27 (Westport, CT: Greenwood Press, 1993), x.

INTRODUCTION

a Christian" and "Living as a Christian"—though for Forsyth these two "moments" blend as what we believe informs how we live as Christians; and how we live as Christians is grounded in what we believe.

The devotions are not strictly, specifically ordered. Forsyth has been called an "unsystematic systematician," meaning Forsyth did not present a "tight" systematic theology in which all questions are answered, all paradoxes resolved, and all "loose ends" are settled. Rather, Forsyth presents theological thoughts, grounded in Scripture, which speak to theological questions and issues that go to the deep places of life and are at the core of the biblical revelation of God's grace to humanity, expressed in Jesus Christ. All Forsyth has to say is part of this whole. His direct speaking and writing focus on central issues of the Christian Gospel.

Jesus Christ came to bring a Gospel, Forsyth believed. It was this Gospel that saw Forsyth through the vicissitudes and difficulties of life. This faith can be our own. As Forsyth summarized it all:

> I should count a life well spent, and the world well lost, if, after testing all its experiences, and facing all its problems, I had no more to show at its close, or carry with me to another life, than the acquisition of a real, pure, humble, and grateful faith in the Eternal and Incarnate Son of God.[5]

May this book deepen Christian understanding and Christian faith!

---

5. P. T. Forsyth, *The Person and Place of Jesus Christ* (London: Hodder & Stoughton, 1909), 255.

Using This Book

THIS IS A BOOK of devotions or reflections on quotations from the Scottish theologian, Peter Taylor Forsyth (1848–1921). Each piece is meant to explain the meaning of the Forsyth quotation and to reflect on the theological meaning of the quotation for the church and for Christian life today. The quotes are drawn from a range of Forsyth's many writings.

Both groups and individuals can use this book. The selections are appropriate for use in various church gatherings. Individuals can use the pieces during times of reflection and devotion.

The book has two Parts: "Believing as a Christian" and "Living as a Christian." The selections in each Part can be used in the order they appear, or randomly.

Several elements can be helpful in using the book.

Read the Devotion. Each piece is written compactly. So each sentence is important. The individual sentences can be a source for reflection as they each are read. After each sentence, pause and reflect on its meaning.

Meditate on the Quotation and Devotion. Questions relating to Forsyth's quotation and the devotion that follow can help focus meditation:

- What is Forsyth saying here?
- What does Forsyth's thought mean for the life of the church?
- What does Forsyth's thought mean for my own life of faith?
- What new or changed attitudes am I led toward through Forsyth's thought?

- What are ways Forsyth's thought can be enacted in the life of the church community and in my own life?

Pray about this devotion. Reflect on your meditations and gather your thoughts into a prayer in which you ask God's Holy Spirit to lead you into ways God wants you to believe and live.

Act on the insights you receive. Decide on ways this devotion can affect your life and begin to put these ways of believing and living into your service for Christ. Reorient ways of living. Follow new directions for your Christian witness according to God's will.

++++

The title of each devotion can be a phrase to bring its key insights to mind. As you review the titles of each devotion, recall the important meanings that emerge from each piece.

If you keep a journal, you can summarize what the quotation/reflection means to you and how it can impact your life. You can periodically review these summaries in the future.

You can also consult titles from the "Selected Resources for Further Reflection" section to read more of Forsyth's works and works about P. T. Forsyth.

BELIEVING AS A CHRISTIAN

1

The Word of God Is the Gospel

> Revelation is not merely the Bible. It is what gives value to the Bible; it is the Gospel in the Bible. It is not a book saying something, but a person doing something.... The Word of God is the Gospel, which is in the Bible, but it is not identical with the Bible.[1]

THERE IS A TERM, "bibliolatry," which literally means "worship of the Bible." It makes the Bible itself an object of excessive reverence or "worship."

Forsyth wanted to make clear that God's revelation through the Bible does not make the Bible itself what is most valuable: it is "the Gospel in the Bible" that is the Word of God. The gospel is the Bible's witness to God doing something—all through history: in Israel and in the church while at work in the world. The Bible's value as God's revelation is not just as a "book saying something." The Word of God that is revealed and comes to us in the Bible is the story of the gospel, centered in Jesus Christ and especially in the cross of Christ.

This keeps our focus on what is most important. Our reverence for the Bible and its value is because of what the Bible conveys—the unique revelation of the God who is holy love and who has come into the world in the person of Jesus Christ. As John 3:16

---

1. P. T. Forsyth, "Revelation and the Bible," *Hibbert Journal*, X (October, 1911), 240. in *The Gospel and Authority*, 81.

puts it: "For God so loved the world that he gave his only Son, so that everyone who believes in him may not perish but may have eternal life." This gospel message is not identical with the Bible itself. But the Bible is our only source for knowing who God is and what God has done in Jesus Christ.

The gospel of Jesus Christ is the gospel given to us in the Bible. The gospel is God's "good news" to us and for us. Let us rejoice and believe the gospel!

2

Christ Came to Bring a Gospel

> The Bible's inspiration, and its infallibility, are such as pertain to redemption and not theology, to salvation and not mere history. It is as infallible as a Gospel requires, not as a system. Remember that Christ did not come to bring a Bible but to bring a Gospel. The Bible arose afterwards from the Gospel to serve the Gospel.[2]

WE KNOW ABOUT JESUS Christ through the Holy Scriptures. The Bible is our only source of the knowledge of Christ—and the knowledge that is most important about Christ: He is the Son of God who came to earth to die for our sins and to be raised for our justification (1 Cor 15:3; Rom 4:25).

Forsyth recognized the Bible is the medium God uses through which Jesus Christ is made known. We know the gospel through the Scriptures. The church and its theologians have spoken of the Bible as "inspired"—by the Holy Spirit. Some theologians used the term "infallible" for Scripture; and have meant different things by it. But for Forsyth, "the Bible's inspiration, and its infallibility, are such as pertain to redemption and not theology, to salvation and not mere history." We do not look to the Bible to learn "history"— but to hear the message of redemption and salvation. The Bible is "infallible" *for this purpose*—it will never lead us astray.

---

2. P. T. Forsyth, *Positive Preaching and Modern Mind* (London: Hodder & Stoughton, 1907; rpt. 1981), 15.

Forsyth continued to say the Bible is "as infallible as a Gospel requires, not as a system. Remember that Christ did not come to bring a Bible but to bring a Gospel. The Bible arose afterwards from the Gospel to serve the Gospel." The Bible presents the story or message of Jesus Christ—the gospel—the "good news" of salvation and new life in Christ. This is exactly what we need. We do not need an historically "perfect" book; we need to know of the savior who died for us. Jesus Christ brought us and gave us himself. For Forsyth, "the Gospel was there before the Bible, and it created the Bible." The Bible is to serve the gospel!

3
God's Initiative of Free Grace

> The first feature of a positive Gospel is that it is a Gospel of pure, free grace to human sin. . . . The initiative rests entirely with God, and with a holy and injured God. On this article of grace the whole of Christianity turns.[3]

THE TRUE, POSITIVE GOSPEL of Jesus Christ is the gospel of God's *grace*.

God's grace is primary because it shows God reaching out to sinful persons. Sinners have offended the God of holy love who comes to this world to transform those who have sinned against this holy love. The cross of Christ is the supreme expression of this action of God—this act of grace.

Forsyth emphasized that this gospel is of God's "pure, free grace" to sinners. God did not *have* to care about sinners, much less, to love them. But of God's own free choice—as pure grace to sinners—God takes the initiative to bring grace to create, in Jesus Christ, a new, transforming relationship between sinners and God. This transformation is not possible by human actions. Sinners cannot remake themselves. We cannot take credit for this grace since grace is what God has given.

Grace is the divine priority. God's initiative of grace brings a living and vital "new life" for sinners in Christ Jesus: "If anyone is in Christ, there is a new creation: everything old has passed away;

---

3. P. T. Forsyth, *Positive Preaching and Modern Mind* (London: Hodder & Stoughton, 1907; rpt. 1981), 212.

see, everything has become new!" (2 Cor 5:17). In a rare autobiographical statement, Forsyth said of his own transformation: "I was turned . . . from a lover of love to an object of grace" (282–83). We do not earn God's grace and forgiveness; grace is freely given to undeserving sinners. Forsyth's faith had "an experimental foundation in grace" (283).

God's grace is the central reality of Christian faith. God freely makes the first move, in Jesus Christ, to transform sinners and make us a new creation!

4
God Gave Us Himself

> What God gave us was neither His portrait nor His principle; He gave us Himself—His presence, His life, His action. He did more than show us Himself; more than teach us about Himself—He gave us Himself, He sacrificed Himself. It is ourselves He seeks, therefore it was Himself He gave, life for life and soul for soul.[4]

Jesus Christ is God's gift to the world. He is God's love in action; and that action was Christ's death on the cross, on behalf of sinners. As Paul put it: "God proves his love for us in that while we still were sinners Christ died for us" (Rom 5:8).

Forsyth was always clear that we know who Jesus Christ *is* by what Jesus Christ has *done*—supremely by his death on the cross. In Christ, God has given us "His presence, His life, His action." In short, God gave us God's own self.

Realizing this keeps our faith in Christ from being either a "portrait" or a "principle."

God's revelation in Christ is not simply a picture, or "portrait," to sketch God's character. That would keep Christ as an object, held at arm's length, to be gazed upon as one would admire an historic person.

---

4. P. T. Forsyth, "Revelation, Old and New" (1911) in *Revelation Old and New: Sermons and Addresses*, ed. John Huxtable (London: Independent, 1962), 10.

Nor, is God's revelation to be a "principle" so Christ is a great communicator about God, telling us what to believe so we can credit Christ with words of wisdom or inspiration.

God draws us to Christ through his death, giving us God's own self: God "sacrificed Himself," said Forsyth. Since "it is ourselves" God seeks, "it was Himself He gave, life for life and soul for soul." Christ died for us. We commit our lives to God because God is committed to us. God "gave us love by giving us Himself to love" (10).

5

A Trinitarian God

> The Father who *spoke* by his prophets must *come* to save in the Son and must *occupy* in the Spirit. He offers, gives, Himself in the Son and conveys Himself in the Spirit. . . . Only on this Trinitarian conception of God can we think of such a salvation as ours. Only so can we think of Christ as God with us.[5]

THE DOCTRINE OF THE Trinity was developed in the early centuries of the Christian church. It expresses what the church believes about who God is and what God does, on the basis of Scripture. The church's elaboration of its belief about God as Trinity—"one God in three persons"—is derived from the whole teachings of Scripture.

The Trinity is foundational for all Christian theology, as it was for the theology of P. T. Forsyth. He did not delve into the "mysteries" of the Trinity and did not carefully develop a doctrine of the Holy Spirit. But Forsyth believed the Trinity was vital for the church and important for Christian belief. Its vitality related to the work of the three persons of the Trinity.

Here, he gives a capsulized view: The Father *spoke*—by the prophets; the Son *came*—to save; the Spirit must *occupy* us. Thus: The Father "offers, gives, Himself in the Son and conveys Himself

---

5. P. T. Forsyth, *The Person and Place of Jesus Christ* (London: Hodder & Stoughton, 1909), 327.

in the Spirit." The three persons are fully involved together in "a salvation such as ours."

The doctrine of the Trinity also ensures we recognize the three persons are fully God and in full communion with each other. This is essential, as Forsyth maintained, to enable us to "think of Christ as God with us."

In the Trinity, we realize that all that God-in-three persons does . . . is done *for us*. God's speaking is *for us* to hear. God's Son came to bring *us* reconciliation and save *us*. God's Spirit abides with *us* and with the church.

God in three persons . . . blessed Trinity!

6

A Gracious God

> The first condition to be satisfied by any doctrine about Christ's person is that it shall be necessary to the central principle of Christianity that "in Christ we have a gracious God."[6]

CHRISTIANITY IS FOCUSED ON Jesus Christ. "Christians" are followers of Christ. Jesus Christ is the crucified and risen savior. Christ is present with the church and in the lives of Christian believers by the power of the Holy Spirit.

The Christian conviction is that in Jesus of Nazareth, God had come among sinful people. Jesus is "Emmanuel," which means, "God is with us" (Matt 1:23). In Jesus Christ, "the Word became flesh and lived among us" (John 1:14).

Forsyth wanted us to realize that our beliefs about Christ's person, who Jesus Christ is, should focus us on "the central principle of Christianity." First and foremost, Christians believe in Jesus Christ; and that in Jesus Christ "we have a gracious God." Jesus reveals God as the gracious God to whom the Psalmist prayed (Pss 86:15; 103:8). Now God has become "incarnate." God has become a person in Jesus himself.

Martin Luther said that when he was a monk, his basic question was: Where do I find a gracious God? Now we know where the gracious God is found. This God is revealed in the person of

---

6. P. T. Forsyth, *The Person and Place of Jesus Christ* (London: Hodder & Stoughton, 1909), 245.

Jesus Christ, who lived among us, died to save us, and was raised for our justification (Rom 4:25).

Jesus reveals the gracious God—this is the "central principle" of Christianity. Through the death and resurrection of Jesus Christ, our sin is forgiven. We are reconciled with God. We are given a new status before God—now living in love and trust in God, by faith. God is gracious, giving us grace, which is purely undeserved by us. New life is ours through Jesus Christ our savior and Lord. Amen!

7

God is Holy Love

> This holiness of God is the real foundation of religion; Love is but its outgoing; sin is but its defiance; grace is but its action on sin; the cross is but its victory; faith is but its worship. This holiness is no attribute of God, but his very essence. The moral is the real. It is not a quality in God, but the being of God, in which all else inheres. God is Holy Love.[7]

In Isaiah's vision in the temple, he heard seraphs (six-winged creatures) calling to each other: "'Holy, holy, holy is the Lord of hosts; the whole earth is full of his glory'" (Isa 6:3). God is holy (Lev 11:44). Being "holy" is a most basic description of God. To be holy is to be set apart, to be completely pure. God being "holy" is at the *core* of who God is.

Forsyth stressed God is holy love. We know "God is love" (1 John 4:8, 16). But God's *holy* love expresses God's holiness as the supreme Lord who is sacred, the One whom all beings worship as "Holy, holy, holy."

Forsyth saw love as the outgoing expression of God's holiness. Sin, by contrast, is human defiance of the holiness of God. We offend God and rebel against God's desire that humans also be holy (Lev 11:45). God's grace is God's action regarding sin where, in the cross of Jesus Christ, sin is forgiven and Christ is victorious

---

7. P. T. Forsyth, "Forgiveness through Atonement," in *Revelation Old and New* (London: Independent, 1962), 62.

over sin. In faith, forgiven sinners worship the God of holy love. We worship God in God's "very essence," said Forsyth. God's holiness means that the "moral is the real" throughout the universe because "the moral order reflects the nature of a holy God" (63). God's "holy love" is not just an attribute—a quality or characteristic—of God. It is, said Forsyth, "the *very being* of God." In this, "all else inheres" and comes together. God is holy love!

8

Sin is Utterly Irrational

> The mystery of iniquity who can understand? Sin is utterly irrational.[8]

WE MAY PRIDE OURSELVES on being "rational" people. We like to think we act on the basis of our rational powers. We solve our problems by making good choices based on having "thought out" the issue. We use logic and reason, which lead us to choose or act. When we don't follow this course, we say we acted "irrationally."

In an intriguing biblical phrase, Paul speaks of "the mystery of iniquity" (KJV; "mystery of lawlessness," NRSV; 2 Thess 2:7). Instead of iniquity or lawlessness being something we rationally consider and then act upon, the apostle speaks of iniquity or sin as a "mystery." Why should we sin? Is sin something we think about first, decide—using our reason—that sin is a good thing to do; and then sin? Why should we sin if we believe sin is against God's will, is bad, and may even be dangerous for us?

Forsyth caught this when he used the biblical phrase and wrote: "The mystery of iniquity who can understand? Sin is utterly irrational." Sin is a mystery. Why we sin is a mystery. Sin is not a "rational" thing to do, according to Christians, given biblical warnings about sin, and our belief that sin is "against" God and what God wills. Sin is "utterly irrational," said Forsyth; and so it is.

---

8. P. T. Forsyth, *God the Holy Father* (London: Independent, 1957), 74. Originally in *The Holy Father and the Living Christ* (London: Hodder & Stoughton, 1897).

Often when we sin, we look back and see what we did was an "utterly irrational" thing to do—given our sin's results or consequences. We may have convinced ourselves, beforehand, this "temptation" is something we want. But we later realize it was not as it seemed; and we should not have done it.

The only remedy for sin is not to justify it or "explain it away." Our only remedy is to confess our sin to God: "If we confess our sins, God is faithful and just and will forgive us our sins and purify us from all unrighteousness" (1 John 1:9).

9

Sin Is Not Our Life-Principle

> But it [i.e., sin] does not reign in us. It is not our life-principle, though it may get expression in our life. We sin, but not unto death. We still have and still use the Advocate with the Father. Against our sin we plant ourselves on God's side.[9]

CHRISTIANS SIN. THIS IS a fact of our Christian existence.

The ultimate power of sin in our lives—the "original sin" we inherited as humans and which held us totally in its grasp—is broken by the victorious work of Jesus Christ on the cross and the salvation we receive by faith as God's gift of grace. But even after we are "saved," we still sin. We will never be "perfect" Christians—sin-free.

Forsyth recognized this. Though we sin, he notes that sin "does not reign in us." Sin is not our "life-principle." As Christians, we do not set out deliberately to pursue sin, even though sin does "get expression in our life." Our sin is serious. But ultimately—because of Christ—it is not sin "unto death." Forsyth went on to say, "there is sin as the principle of a soul and sin as an incident, sin which stays and sin which visits" (45). Even after we are justified by faith (Rom 5:1), we will have "visitations of sin," which affect our new life in Christ. While we have freedom to sin, sin is to be avoided. We have constant need of "daily forgiveness" (45).

---

9. P. T. Forsyth, *Christian Perfection* (London: Hodder & Stoughton, 1899), 37.

Given this, Forsyth reminds us that "we still have and still use the Advocate with the Father." He is recalling the promise that "if anyone does sin, we have an advocate with the Father, Jesus Christ the righteous" (1 John 2:1). God has forgiven and continues to forgive us as Jesus Christ intercedes and advocates for us. Our prayers for forgiveness through Jesus Christ express our desire that "against our sin," we "plant ourselves on God's side."

10

Christ Came to Effect Forgiveness

> Christ came not to *say* something, but to *do* something. His revelation was action more than instruction. He revealed by redeeming. The thing He did was not simply to make us aware of God's disposition in an impressive way. It was not to *declare* forgiveness. It was certainly not to *explain* forgiveness. And it was not even to *bestow* forgiveness. It was to *effect* forgiveness, to set up the relation of forgiveness both in God and man.[10]

When we read the New Testament, we are struck by what Jesus said; and by what Jesus did.

Words and actions always go together in some fashion. Jesus certainly came to speak to us—he was the (Gr.) *logos*—the "Word" (John 1:1).

But Forsyth wanted to stress that "Christ came not to *say* something, but to *do* something. His revelation was action more than instruction." Jesus' words led to the cross, the place where Jesus *did* something no one else could do. He died for our sins and to give us new life in communion with God (Eph 1:7).

Christ's death brought forgiveness of our sin. Jesus' death was more than simply an "explanation" that our sin can now be forgiven. His death was not to provide a detailed discussion to tell us how forgiveness happens. Jesus' action was much more. Jesus

---

10. P. T. Forsyth, *The Holy Father* (London: Independent, 1957), 19. Originally in *The Holy Father and the Living Christ* (London: Hodder & Stoughton, 1897).

did not bestow forgiveness—like someone handing out gifts on a street-corner.

Jesus' death was, said Forsyth, "to *effect* forgiveness, to set up the relation of forgiveness both in God and man." God forgives our sin in Christ. We receive forgiveness and the new relationship of faith which Jesus' death makes possible. Forsyth went on to say Christ's death "set up no new affection in God, but a new and creative relation on both sides of the spiritual world" (20). It gave us "a new relation to God, and God, a new relation, though not a new feeling" to us (20). Christ makes forgiveness happen!

11

The Kingdom Breaking In

> The Cross of Christ is not the preliminary of the Kingdom; it is the Kingdom breaking in. It is not the clearing of the site for the heavenly city; it is the city itself descending out of heaven from God.[11]

WHEN WE THINK OF the "kingdom of God," we may think of the coming future: God's reign will be perfect and "heaven," a reality.

This dimension of the "kingdom of God (heaven)" is certainly true. We anticipate when "'The kingdom of the world has become the kingdom of our Lord and of his Messiah, and he will reign forever and ever'" (Rev 11:15).

But there is more.

God's kingdom and reign has already broken into our world. Forsyth sees this happening in the cross of Jesus Christ. The cross as the climax of Jesus' life and work is the crucial action that signals God's kingdom is here. As Forsyth said: "It is not the clearing of the site for the heavenly city; it is the city itself descending out of heaven from God." The kingdom is "actually set up in the cross" (81). There, Christ absorbed God's judgment on human sin so God's purposes could be carried out, "whose purpose is the world's salvation to Himself in a kingdom" (44). It is from God's love and for God's kingdom "for which we are saved" (75).

---

11. P. T. Forsyth, *The Justification of God* (New York: Charles Scribner's Sons, 1917), 75.

Christ's cross is the critical component of "a universal Kingdom of peace and joy to the glory of the holy name" (136). The "final goal of the Kingdom" is "the deepest of all forces in history" (161). We know God's kingdom has broken into the world, now. We experience it in Jesus Christ. His cross judges our sin and liberates us for salvation to be Christ's disciples. Forsyth says: "The kingdom is above all a gift, but it is also a conquest. We are here to fight the good fight rather than to have a good time" (217)!

12

What Is Faith?

> The mystery and the power of Christianity is faith—understood not merely as a religious sympathy or affection, but as direct, personal communion with Christ, based on forgiveness of sins direct from Him to the conscience.[12]

"Faith" is a word we use in many ways. We may say we have "faith in the brakes of our car." Or, we have "faith our favorite team will win." But what does faith mean in our Christian faith?

Forsyth focused on the centrality of faith. He said faith was "the mystery and the power of Christianity." Christianity is fixed on faith—a conviction about someone: God in Jesus Christ. Faith has an "object"; and that "object" is a person: Jesus Christ.

Faith is in Jesus Christ, not in Jesus as an historical figure or someone we admire. Faith is a "direct, personal communion with Christ, based on forgiveness of sins direct from Him to the conscience." There is an immediacy to faith; and that is an immediate, direct "personal communion with Christ"—who was crucified, raised from the dead, and now "lives by the power of God" (2 Cor 13:4).

Communion with Christ, for believers, is based on Christ's death for the forgiveness of sins (Col 1:14). We are united with Christ by faith and experience a direct relationship of communion with him. Faith is the means by which we know Jesus Christ today.

---

12. P. T. Forsyth, *Rome, Reform and Reaction: Four Lectures on the Religious Situation* (London: Hodder and Stoughton, 1899), 92–93.

We can be as conscious of Jesus Christ as of any living person with whom we communicate, or as of any reality. Through faith we experience the reality of Christ's presence in our lives. We live in a relationship of love and trust in Christ who is alive in us by the power of God's Spirit. "There must be," as Forsyth wrote, "personal contact, personal experience, personal faith" (104). Faith is personal communion with Christ!

13

The Work of the Holy Spirit

> The ministry of the Word is the chief agency of the Holy Ghost, and the chief function of the Church; whose business is not simply publication of a truth but confession of an experience—the experience of the indwelling Spirit as its life. It is the Holy Spirit that makes the Word to be revelation; it is the Word that makes revelation historic and concrete.[13]

IN PROTESTANT THEOLOGY GOD'S "Word" and God's "Spirit" go together.

God's Word in Scripture is the means through which we know who God is and what God has done. God's Spirit brings Scripture alive and makes it authoritative in our lives. The Spirit enables us to interpret the Word; and the Word helps us recognize what the Spirit says to us.

Forsyth points in these directions when he links Word and Spirit. The Word is "the chief agency" of the Spirit and "the chief function of the Church." The Word is central.

The Spirit makes Scripture "to be revelation" for us, giving us the experience of the presence or "indwelling" of the Spirit in our lives. Scripture becomes experiential for us—leading us in God's will and way: "Your word is a lamp to my feet and a light to my path" (Ps 119:105). God's revelation is "historic and concrete." The

---

13. P. T. Forsyth, *Faith, Freedom, and the Future* (London: Hodder & Stoughton, 1912), 15.

indwelling of the Spirit enables us to experience God's revelation—which the church proclaims.

The work of the Holy Spirit is vital in helping us know what to believe and how to live. The Word shows us God's will. The Spirit, who helps us interpret Scripture, never leads us in ways counter to God's will. The Spirit leads the church—and disciples of Jesus Christ—into ways of ministry. The Spirit within us is always with us, uniting us with Jesus Christ by faith and sustaining us by being the church's life in all ways.

14

The Spirit Brings Regeneration

> In the New Testament the Holy Spirit, the Lord the Spirit, is an objective power, working, before all sanctification, a new creation, and effecting it from the focal point of the Cross and Resurrection, and the thing done there once for all. It is not the spirit of discipleship but of regeneration by that Word.[14]

IN THE NEW TESTAMENT, the Holy Spirit does many things. The Holy Spirit is one of the three persons of the Godhead, with the Father and the Son. Each member is fully God. All are equal in power and glory. But each member has functions to carry out in the whole work of God as described in Scripture.

The Holy Spirit carries out many activities. Forsyth indicates the Holy Spirit brings "regeneration" by the Word of God. Regeneration means "new birth" or "new life." The Holy Spirit transforms sinful persons by giving them the gift of faith in Jesus Christ so they experience being "born from above," as Jesus said (John 3:7); and salvation in Jesus Christ (Titus 3:5).

The Holy Spirit makes us a "new creation." "Everything old has passed away; see, everything has become new!" proclaimed Paul (2 Cor 5:17). This is "regeneration," a new life in Christ Jesus.

Forsyth notes this regenerative action of the Holy Spirit precedes the Spirit's work in "sanctification" or helping us grow in

---

14. P. T. Forsyth, *Faith, Freedom, and the Future* (London: Hodder & Stoughton, 1912), 13.

grace throughout our Christian lives. The Spirit regenerates us by illuminating us to receive what Jesus Christ did in his death on the cross and his resurrection. These two events in the life of Christ, done once and for all, are the "focal point" from which our new birth, our new life—our salvation—comes. The Spirit's work is to point us to Christ's death and resurrection and enable us to receive forgiveness for our sins by giving us the gift of faith in Christ. Our salvation by God's grace is through the work of the Holy Spirit!

15

Christ Was Born to Die

> The Cross is there as the agent of God's grace in redemption. Christ was born to die. To preach Christ really means to preach the Cross where His person took effect as the incarnation and the agent of the atoning grace of God.[15]

THEOLOGIANS HAVE LONG DEBATED the question: (Lat.) *Cur Deus Homo?* Or "Why [did] God [become] human?" This relates to the doctrine of the incarnation. Why did Jesus Christ, the second person of the Trinity—the "Word" of God (John 1:1) become a human person? As John puts it: "The Word became flesh and lived among us" (1:14).

Anselm of Canterbury (c. 1033–1109) wrote a book with this title in 1098. His answer to the question was that Jesus became a human person to die for the sin of the world. This was the purpose of his incarnation.

Forsyth agreed. For him, the cross was central to Christianity and stands as "the agent of God's grace in redemption." It is through the cross of Christ that salvation comes to the world. So "Christ was born to die." This was the work of Christ. Forsyth said that Christ was "gathered up for us, as for God, in the consummation of the Cross" (22).

---

15. P. T. Forsyth, *Positive Preaching and Modern Mind* (London: Hodder & Stoughton, 1907; rpt. 1981), 22.

This is the church's belief and is the core of Christian preaching, said Forsyth. For "to preach Christ really means to preach the Cross where His person took effect as the incarnation and the agent of the atoning grace of God." On the cross, the Son of God carried out the work of salvation, making atonement for human sin, and bringing the grace of God to the world. Christ died to save us. As Forsyth continued: "Christ Himself existed—not to present us with the supreme spiritual spectacle of history, but to achieve the critical thing in history" (22). The crucified Christ *achieved salvation*: "The Gospel means something done and not simply declared" (22). Christ was born to die!

16

What Love!

> The divine Father is the holy. And the Holy Father's first care is holiness. The first charge on a Redeemer is satisfaction to that holiness. The Holy Father is one who does and must atone. . . . Fatherhood is not bought from holiness by any cross; it is holiness itself that pays. It is love that expiates. Do not say, "God is love. Why atone?" The New Testament says, "God has atoned. What love!" The ruling passion of the Saviour's holy God is this passion to atone and to redeem.[16]

WHATEVER ELSE IS SAID about God, a first thing to say is that "God is holy." This theme resonates throughout the Bible, with God declaring: "you shall be holy, for I am holy" (Lev 11:45; 1 Pet 1:16).

Forsyth spoke of God as the "Holy Father" and God's love as "God's holy love." He believed that primarily God is holy. And the One who will redeem unholy, sinful people is to satisfy the divine desire for people to be holy by atoning for their sin. God provides for this atonement by the sending of a holy redeemer so forgiveness and reconciliation can occur. In sending Jesus Christ, atonement for sin is made—through Christ's death on the cross. There, God's holiness is expiated and God and humanity are brought "at-one."

This atonement in Jesus Christ leaves us astounded: "God has atoned. What love!" God has dealt with the most basic problem of human existence: sin against the holy God. We know God is love

---

16. P. T. Forsyth, *God the Holy Father* (London: Independent, 1955), 4. Originally in *The Holy Father and the Living Christ* (1897).

because atonement has been made in Jesus Christ! Forsyth says, "The ruling, passion of the Saviour's holy God is this passion to atone and to redeem."

What greater love could we imagine? Our Holy Father atones for our sinfulness and offense against the God of holy love—by sending God's own Son to die for us. This is the deepest love. This is God's passion to redeem and reconcile sinners . . . what love!

17

Atonement Makes Repentance

> The past cannot be erased, cannot be altered, cannot be repaired. There it stands. It can only be atoned; and never by us. If our repentance atoned, it would lose the humility which makes it worth most. It is atonement that makes repentance, not repentance that makes atonement.[17]

WE ALL HAVE REGRETS. We are sorry for things we wish we had not done. We have brought harm, sadness, or broken relationships—with others; and with God. Memories haunt us. Forsyth said, "the past cannot be erased, cannot be altered, cannot be repaired. There it stands." So it does.

Then Forsyth wrote: "It can only be atoned; and never by us." We need atonement—forgiveness for our wrongs. But we can never do the "atoning." We have no power to atone and forgive our pasts, no matter how hard we try. Before God, we cannot "repent" or be sorry for our sins—to make them "go away." For "we may sorrow and amend, but we cannot atone and reconcile" (17).

Only God can forgive us. If our repentance could atone, "it would lose humility which makes it worth most." If we say we can "repent" and make all things right—then we would not be *humbly* sorry—we would be asserting ourselves and simply declaring all is well. No humility here!

---

17. P. T. Forsyth, *God the Holy Father* (London: Independent, 1955), 11. Originally in *The Holy Father and the Living Christ* (1897).

So, Forsyth rightly says: "It is atonement that makes repentance, not repentance that makes atonement." God acts to forgive us, through the cross of Jesus Christ. That forgiveness is atonement. Forgiveness and reconciliation are given by God, against whom we have sinned. God sent Christ as atonement for our sins. He is our forgiveness. We "repent" when we confess our sin, express sorrow, and then live in new ways of obedience to God. Atonement leads us to repent . . . out of profound gratitude!

18

Kingdom—Act and Gift of God

> We do not contribute to the Kingdom, we only work out a Kingdom which is ours wholly because our God works it in. The central thing in the Kingdom is not a state, nor a feeling, nor an act of ours, but it is an act and gift of God.[18]

FORSYTH WROTE THAT "THERE is nothing so prominent in Christ's teaching as the Kingdom of God" (92). Forsyth, said the kingdom of God was "at once supernatural and ethical, nor only present and future at once, come and coming; it is also both a relation to God and a society of God" (91). Jesus taught about the kingdom when he said, "the kingdom of heaven is like . . ." (Matt 13:44, 45, 47, etc.). He proclaimed its presence when he said: "the kingdom of God is among you." (Luke 17:21). He also taught to anticipate the fullness of the coming kingdom: "Your kingdom come" (Matt 6:10).

But for Jesus, "about that Kingdom there was nothing to His mind so sure as that it was the gift of God. It came to the world from His grace, and not from effort of ours" (92). God initiates and enacts the kingdom: "We do not contribute to the Kingdom, we only work out a Kingdom which is ours wholly because our God works it in." Or, we can say: The kingdom is not ours to win; it's God's to give.

18. P. T. Forsyth, *The Church and the Sacraments*, 3rd ed. (London: Independent, 1949 [1917]), 92.

Forsyth emphasized that "the central thing in the Kingdom is not a state, nor a feeling, nor an act of ours, but it is an act and gift of God." God acts to initiate the kingdom in Jesus Christ. Christ's cross, Forsyth believed, was where God's kingdom was established in the great act of forgiveness and reconciliation effected for the world in Jesus Christ.

God's act is God's gift. The kingdom of God is given to the world, not from human deserving but from the depths of God's holy love.

19

From Hostility to Peace

> By reconciliation Paul meant the total result of Christ's life-work in the fundamental, permanent, final changing of the relation between man and God, altering it from a relation of hostility to one of confidence and peace.[19]

FORSYTH BELIEVED GOD'S RECONCILIATION of the world in Jesus Christ (2 Cor 5:14—6:2) was the great "backbone of the Church." Christ's death on the cross permanently changed the relation between all humanity and God. This reconciliation was the "total result of Christ's life-work," which brought a "fundamental, permanent," and "final" change to the human-divine relationship.

Forsyth stressed the collective here. He said he was speaking "as Paul spoke," about humanity itself and not about individual persons or groups of persons.

In Jesus Christ, God "covered" the sin of humanity in an "atonement." This act of Christ makes sin lose its power of derailing the covenant relationship between God and humanity. The effect of Christ's death as the universal atonement for human sin is that a "new humanity" is formed. The effect, in other words, is to shift the status of the human race from an attitude and relationship of "hostility" toward God—the result of human sin since the beginning of the race; to a new relationship of "peace"—the peace that is grounded in Jesus Christ (Eph 2:14–15). The new humanity

---

19. P. T. Forsyth, *The Work of Christ* (London: Hodder & Stoughton, 1910), 54.

is reconciled to God; and to one another in Jesus Christ so hostility is at an end (2:16).

This astounding message of reconciliation is the Christian gospel. "Reconciliation" is Paul's "great characteristic word and thought" (56). The reconciling act of God in Jesus Christ is not merely a gesture or a showing of the world how much God loved them. Instead, reconciliation is an "act." "Reconciliation must rest on atonement," said Forsyth (57). Christ took human sins on himself so they are no longer "counted against us" (2 Cor 5:19). Christ took on the sin of "the whole human race as one whole" (57). This changes the relationship from "alienation" to "communion"—"reciprocal communion" between God and humanity (57): from hostility to peace!

20

Judgment Comes Down in Mercy

> There is no such majesty conceivable as the holiness of God; and in Christ's Cross, its judgment all comes down in mercy.[20]

CENTRAL TO THE CHRISTIAN faith is the conviction that humans do not find their way to God; but God comes to the world in God's eternal Son, Jesus Christ. God is revealed in Christ (John 1:14). Revelation moves from God to the world. Or, as Forsyth put it, "We cannot find Him in His world, and He must find us" (20).

The God who is revealed is "the Almighty." But God is also "the All Holy." This, said Forsyth is "a dreadful, crushing revelation, unless the holy God is revealed also as the God of all grace; unless revelation be redemption" (20). God's "holiness" makes us unworthy to approach God or to stand in God's presence. This is humanity's great dread and fear.

Yet, said Forsyth, "nothing is so miraculous in Christ as that union of infinite majesty and intimate mercy" (20). In Jesus Christ, God has come to the world. The Almighty God who is all-holy comes in the person of Jesus Christ. In his cross we see that Christ comes in intimate mercy! As Forsyth put it: "There is no such majesty conceivable as the holiness of God; and in Christ's Cross, its judgment all comes down in mercy."

---

20. P. T. Forsyth, "Revelation, Old and New," in *Revelation Old and New: Sermons and Addresses*, ed. John Huxtable (London: Independent, 1962), 21.

Imagine! The almighty, holy God, who can judge the world by its sinfulness, by its offense to God's holiness, its sinfulness—this almighty, all-holy God *does* judge the world; but God judges the world in the cross of Jesus Christ... *in mercy!* God's "judgment all comes down in mercy": "infinite majesty and intimate mercy!"

In our hours of guilt and despair over our sin, nothing can reach us except that God's "holiness" is also our "redemption." God comes in "perfect holiness in the Cross of Christ" to save us and quiet us (22)!

21

Atonement Flowed from Grace

> Procured grace is a contradiction in terms. The atonement did not procure grace, it flowed from grace. What was historically offered to God was also eternally offered by God, within the Godhead's unity. The Redeemer was God's gift.[21]

HERE'S A PHRASE TO make you stop and think. Forsyth wrote: "Procured grace is a contradiction in terms." What does this mean? Well, theologically, "grace" means "unmerited favor." Grace is granted, given by God, as a pure divine action—without any human action or achievement causing grace to be given. "Procured grace" contradicts this. If someone "procures" something, it is usually considered as something obtained and acquired by the person. It is not a "gift" but an attainment!

So "procured grace is a contradiction in terms," said Forsyth. In a theological context, grace is given by God; not obtained or attained by a sinful person. In the death of Christ, atonement for sin was gained by Christ. This act, which brings forgiveness of sins, was a gift of God's divine grace. Forsyth said, "The atonement did not procure grace, it flowed from grace."

This is a very key theological point. Our salvation, in Jesus Christ, comes from God's act of grace in sending Christ to die for our sin and provide eternal life (John 3:16). We cannot reverse

---

21. P. T. Forsyth, *The Cruciality of the Cross* (London: Hodder & Stoughton, 1909), 78.

this to say that Christ's death procured or achieved grace. Rather, it is God's grace that led to Christ's death as the means of atonement—forgiveness of sins—and as the way in which eternal life is given. It is God who was in Christ and who, in Christ, provided reconciliation and forgiveness of sins through the atoning death of Jesus (2 Cor 5:19).

God initiates salvation and provides salvation. God's grace brings salvation as a free gift, not as an achievement from humans, or even from Jesus himself. Jesus did not have to induce God to forgive. Jesus, the redeemer, "was God's *gift.*" Salvation is by God's grace in Jesus Christ!

22

Speaking Faith

> Revelation did not come in a statement, but in a person; yet stated it must be. Faith must go on to specify. It must be capable of statement, else it could not spread; for it is not an ineffable incommunicable mysticism.[22]

WHEN WE THINK OF the "revelation of God," we may think of it in various ways. We may think of Scripture as God's revelation; or the work of the Holy Spirit as being what God has revealed. First and foremost, however, we think of Jesus Christ.

We hear Forsyth when he wrote that "revelation did not come in a statement, but in a person." There is no substitute for Jesus. All our words *about* Jesus do not take the place of Jesus himself as "the Word made flesh" who "lived among us" and died to save us. In Jesus Christ, God is revealed in a human person.

Yet Forsyth went on to say that while God's revelation is in the person of Jesus Christ, "yet stated it must be. Faith must go on to specify. It must be capable of statement, else it could not spread; for it is not an ineffable incommunicable mysticism."

If we are to affirm who Jesus is and what Jesus did . . . we need words. Our faith convictions about Jesus Christ must be expressed in human language. It belongs to Christian faith to express itself. Words are necessary to say what we believe; and also to confess our faith in Jesus Christ to other people. Without verbal expressions of

---

22. P. T. Forsyth, *The Person and Place of Jesus Christ* (London: Independent, 1909; rpt. 1955), 15.

the gospel story of Jesus Christ, Christian faith could not spread—in the days of the early church, or today!

We do not look inward to ourselves and focus on our experience of Jesus, in a kind of "mysticism" in a direct apprehension of our savior. We must be able to proclaim Jesus and our experience of Jesus in words that can be shared and become meaningful to others, by the work of the Holy Spirit.

23
God's Message Is God's Own Self

> The Gospel as God's message is His own redemptive act, is prior to any Gospel as man's message of that act. The Gospel is not a revelation about the Cross; it is the Cross as revelation. God's message is the gift of Himself, and not of anything about Himself. It is God Himself in Christ, reconciling; it is not a report that reconciliation has been made.[23]

THE GOSPEL MESSAGE CENTERS in Jesus Christ and what Christ has done through his death on the cross. Christ's death is the redemptive act by which reconciliation of God and sinful humans is accomplished. It is in the cross of Christ that God is revealed in Christ. God's revelation in Christ is the gift of God's own self.

We need always to focus on the events of the gospel message, even as we express the meanings of these events in the words we speak. Forsyth wanted to emphasize that the cross of Jesus Christ is the revelation of God. In the cross, God gave God's own self to the world in the person of the Son of God who loved us and gave himself for us (Gal 2:20). The message of the gospel is the gift of God's self to bring atonement, reconciliation—the forgiveness of sins and the new relationship humans have with God.

No formulations of human words—important as they are—can substitute for the reality of God's own self given for the world's

---

23. P. T. Forsyth, "The Need for a Positive Gospel," *London Quarterly Review* 101 (January 1904), 83.

sin on the cross of Christ. The reality of this reconciliation in Christ is the means of salvation. Our human formulations cannot replace the actuality of what Christ has done in the cross.

No human formulations can exhaust or fully explain the cross as revelation. The full giving of God's self in the death of Jesus Christ reveals God's redemptive act. This act of God's self is "prior to any Gospel" as a human message about that act. Our focus is on the cross where God in Christ reconciled the world!

24

Faith *Is* Salvation

> Faith *is* Salvation; it is not rewarded with Salvation. To be forgiven much is to love much and live anew. The new life is the faith which constantly takes home forgiveness, regeneration, reconciliation, and all they imply for the heart.[24]

ONE OF THE WATCHWORDS of the sixteenth-century Protestant Reformation was *sola fide*—"by faith alone." The emphasis was that God's salvation in Jesus Christ comes by faith. We are not saved by doing "good works" or by combining good works with faith. Salvation is by "faith alone." Faith in Jesus Christ as God's Son and our savior is the only means of salvation. Faith alone saves.

Forsyth said, "faith *is salvation*; it is not rewarded with Salvation." Faith itself is not a "good work" that merits God's favor or salvation. Faith in Jesus brings forgiveness of sins and salvation in Christ. This faith resulting in forgiveness will lead us "to love much and live anew." Forgiveness and new life (regeneration, said Forsyth) are the work of God's Holy Spirit in giving salvation.

The "new life" faith brings as salvation is the faith that leads us to focus on love. It includes "forgiveness, regeneration, reconciliation, and all they imply for the heart," according to Forsyth. No wonder Forsyth can say: "Faith *is* Salvation!" Faith in Jesus Christ brings so much with it!

---

24. P. T. Forsyth, *The Church and the Sacraments*, 3rd ed. (London: Independent, 1949 [1917]), 199.

By faith, we receive forgiveness of sins and thus a new relationship with God. We become new persons in regeneration, "new creations" (2 Cor 5:17) who live now in love for others and service to Christ. By faith we receive the gift of reconciliation, so we are friends again with God . . . and with others. The fullness of salvation is ours through faith.

The theological terms: forgiveness, regeneration, reconciliation have deep meanings for us. They have implications for our hearts—as the fullness of salvation expresses itself within us and without, as we live as God's new people!

25

The Church's One Foundation

> The Church's one foundation, and the trust of its ministry, is not simply Christ, but Christ crucified. . . . The Church rests on the Grace of God, the judging, atoning, regenerating Grace of God, which is His holy Love in the form it must take with human sin. Wherever that is heartily confessed, and goes on to rule, we have the true Church.[25]

THE FOUNDATION OF THE church of Jesus Christ is Jesus Christ crucified. Or, as Forsyth put it: Christ's person "as our Eternal Redeemer in His blood." Christ crucified is what Christ did to create and establish all who came after him as being part of his body, the church (1 Cor 12:27).

Forsyth's emphasis is on Christ's action in the crucifixion and all its effects. Christ crucified (1 Cor 1:23) was an act of the grace of God. God provided the means by which human sin can be forgiven and reconciliation of the world to God was established. Christ crucified was God who, in holy love, expressed "judging, atoning, regenerating" grace to enable human sin to be dealt with in forgiveness. Sin against the holy God could not be overlooked or forgotten. It had to be judged and atoned for so sinful humans can be regenerated—made new creations in Christ Jesus (2 Cor

---

25. P. T. Forsyth, *The Church and the Sacraments*, 3rd ed. (London: Independent, 1949 [1917]), 34.

5:17). All this is by God's grace, God acting in "holy Love in the form it must take with human sin."

Where Christ crucified is recognized as this act of God's grace with all its meanings and this is "heartily confessed, and goes on to rule" in peoples' hearts, "we have the true Church." The church is not created by human words, or deeds, or actions. The church is "a new creation of God in the Holy Spirit." The church's origin is with God's grace. The church's one foundation is Jesus Christ and him crucified!

26

One Church in Various Places

> What the Apostles planted was not Churches but stations of the Church. What the Gospel created was not a crowd of Churches but the one Church in various places. What we have everywhere is the one Church of Christ put down here and there.[26]

WE ARE USED TO seeing churches throughout our communities. They vary in architecture, size, worship styles, and denomination. They are all "local churches," established by Christians, and each seeing itself as a "church."

This multiplicity of churches around us can obscure the fact that there is *one* church of Jesus Christ. As Paul put it, "the body is one and has many members" (1 Cor 12:12). Despite our diversities, were are "all one" in Christ Jesus, our Lord (Gal 3:28).

Forsyth pointed to this when he wrote that "what the Apostles planted was not Churches but stations of the Church. What the gospel created was not a crowd of Churches but the one Church in various places. What we have everywhere is the one Church of Christ put down here and there." The one church exists in various locations. Theologically, each local expression of the church should recognize there is "one Lord, one faith, one baptism" (Eph 4:5).

---

26. P. T. Forsyth, *The Church and the Sacraments*, 3rd ed. (London: Independent, 1949 [1917]), 68.

Forsyth went on to say about the early church: "Wherever you went it did not matter, you went to *the* one *Church*. A member here was a member everywhere. Wherever you had the Word and Spirit of God you had not a Church but *the* Church. The localness was a mere matter of convenience, not of doctrine" (69).

In our days of diversities, it is important to look beyond the various local differences to "the one church" that transcends all differences of true Christians to affirm we are all "one in Christ Jesus" (Gal. 3:28). Wherever we go, we share in the "communion of saints" (Apostles' Creed) in the fellowship of the one church of Jesus Christ our Lord.

27

Enter Christ, Enter the Church

> To be a Christian is not to attach one's salvation to a grand individual, but it is to enter Christ; and to enter Christ is in the same act to enter the Church which is in Christ. Faith in Christ is faith in One Whose indwelling makes a Church, and Who carries a Church within His corporate Person.[27]

SOMETIMES THOSE WHO BECOME Christians think they can set out on the Christian life alone, without the need for others. This includes, without a need for the church. They see the church as an "option" in their Christian lives.

But, theologically, our confession of Jesus Christ as our Lord and savior immediately makes us a part of the body of Christ (1 Cor 12:27), the church. Forsyth spoke clearly on this when he wrote that "to be a Christian is not to attach one's salvation to a grand individual, but it is to enter Christ; and to enter Christ is in the same act to enter the Church which is in Christ. Faith in Christ is faith in One Whose indwelling makes a Church, and Who carries a Church within His corporate Person." To enter "into Christ" is to enter "into the church." Faith in Christ entails faith in the One who embraces all Christian believers within himself as a corporate body—members of the church. Forsyth went on to say that "the same act which sets us in Christ sets us also in the society of

---

27. P. T. Forsyth, *The Church and the Sacraments*, 3rd ed. (London: Independent, 1949 [1917]), 43.

Christ" and "to be in Christ is in the same act to be in the Church" (61, 62).

So the church is not an "option" in our Christian lives. The church is an *absolute necessity!* It is necessary because to be "in Christ" *is* to be "in the church." The outward, visible church bodies we see around us are recognitions of this theological reality. If we do not associate ourselves with fellow, believing Christians in a visible church body, we are not clearly understanding or living out that to which faith in Jesus Christ calls us.

28

Pardon Is New Birth

> Pardon is not the cure of a passing illness, but a new birth in which the whole constitution is changed.[28]

THE CHRISTIAN CHURCH, INCLUDING P. T. Forsyth, has taken sin seriously. Sin ruptures the human relationship with God; breaks God's law; is falling short of God's will for humans. Sin is unholiness in the face of God's holiness.

Sin is serious and has far-reaching effects. Forsyth said, "The whole nature is affected by it, and always." Starkly: "It was I who, at my will's centre, did that thing. It was my will and self that was put into it. My act was not the freak of some point on my circumference. It came from my centre. It was my unitary, indivisible self that was involved and is infected." Our pervasive sin emerges from the core of ourselves, "my will's centre." The human will bends away from God's will to our will. Sin is not accidental mistakes, it comes from our self's center. My *self*, sins. Sin infects our whole existence. Forsyth could have quoted the Psalmist: "O LORD, pardon my guilt, for it is great" (Ps. 25:11).

This is why Forsyth commented that "pardon is not the cure of a passing illness, but a new birth in which the whole constitution is changed." We need God's pardon and forgiveness for our sinfulness, which is a corruption at the core—in our very deepest

---

28. P. T. Forsyth, *Christian Perfection* (London: Hodder & Stoughton, 1899), 6.

selves. Our whole selves need a complete conversion, a revolution of the self. We need a new birth!

Pardon comes in Jesus Christ, in his atonement for our sin. In the gift of faith we receive reconciliation and a new relationship with God. We become a new person, our whole self is changed. We become persons of faith. We are forgiven through Christ—often and much. "The very nature of faith is trust of a Saviour," wrote Forsyth. "It is trust for forgiveness, for forgiveness not only of the old life but of the new." Now, in our new life, we continually need God's pardon. This life of faith, says Forsyth, is "only what it is by reason of grace." Pardon is new birth!

29

Love Is Faith in Its Perfect Form

> Love is but faith in its supreme and perfect form. It is the impassioned expression on the face of faith. There is but one attitude of conformity to the will of God, and that is faith: a faith that, being itself an act of will and obedience, always works outward into love.[29]

WHEN WE THINK OF our relationship to the will of God, we know we want to do God's will. This is basic for us as Christians. We want to follow in the way of Jesus, to do what God reveals to us in the law of God, and to live as God wants us to live as disciples of Jesus Christ as we love God with all that is in us.

Our basic attitude in relation to the will of God is faith. Love is the outward expression of faith. Faith is our attitude: we believe in God and in faith we choose to obey God and God's will in all ways. Our faith-beliefs express our desires to be obedient to God. As we obey God, we find our faith expresses itself in love: to God and to others. As Paul writes, what counts is "faith working through love" (Gal 5:6).

Forsyth put it this way: "Love is but faith in its supreme and perfect form. It is the impassioned expression on the face of faith. There is but one attitude of conformity to the will of God, and that is faith: a faith that, being itself an act of will and obedience, always works outward into love."

---

29. P. T. Forsyth, *Christian Perfection* (London: Hodder & Stoughton, 1899), 5.

Faith focuses on believing God and desiring to do God's will. As we live in this faith, we will find faith "has a face"—and that "face" is love. It is the love that describes our relationship to God. We love the One who "first loved us" (1 John 4:19).

Faith is, Forsyth says, "the sinner's trust in God the Redeemer." Our trust as faith in our redeemer expresses itself supremely in love to God and to all others.

30

Begin with the Grace of God

> In a Christian faith we descend on creation from redemption, we do not descend on redemption from creation, on grace from nature, on faith from science. It is in the Grace of God that all our thought begins.[30]

WHEN WE THINK OF our Christian faith, where does our thought begin? Does it begin with the universe—the vast and unseen reality in which our lives are set? Does it begin with the world around us in all its complexities of nature; and of the humans who inhabit it? Or, perhaps there is another "starting point." Forsyth recognized people can begin from different perspectives. He said, "This is the real crux. Everything does turn on our footing, on our starting point, our notion of reality" (178).

Forsyth maintained that for the Christian: "It is in the Grace of God that all our thought begins." There is a difference between believing in "a God" and believing in the God of grace we know through "the evangelical experience." One can be "religious" by believing in "a God"—even a God who has "created" all things. But to be Christian, according to Forsyth, is to recognize that "beneath, behind, and above God the Creator is God the redeemer."

Forsyth believed that "in a Christian faith we descend on creation from redemption, we do not descend on redemption from creation, on grace from nature, on faith from science. It is in the

---

30. P. T. Forsyth, *The Principle of Authority in Relation to Certainty, Sanctity and Society* (London: Independent, 1913; 2nd ed. 1952), 184.

Grace of God that all our thought begins." The grace of God is the starting point for our view of reality. This grace is known in the cross of Jesus Christ. Sinful humanity's "central experience is Grace." This is the reality of a moral universe where we know "the supreme revelation of the Crucified." The "ground plan" of creation and of all being is "God's redemptive Will" in the cross of Jesus Christ. "All our thought"—and all reality—begins with the grace of God.

31

Ministry as Evangelical Succession

> What the ministry had was a functional continuity in preaching the Word revealed to the Apostles, administering its Sacraments, and applying its principles in a Christian ethic. The Apostolic succession is the Evangelical succession. Its continuity lies not in a due devolution but in a common inspiration, a common ministration of God's grace as mercy.[31]

CHRISTIAN MINISTRY TODAY HAS a continuity with the ministries of Christians in the early church. Some traditions speak of an "apostolic succession" and seek to trace back historic roots from contemporary times to the apostles.

The Protestant tradition has seen ministry in the tradition and succession to the apostles to relate to the continual preaching and teaching of the Word of God. Some have spoken of this as "the sacrament of the Word."

Forsyth stands in this tradition by stressing "a functional continuity in preaching the Word revealed to the Apostles, administering its Sacraments, and applying its principles in a Christian ethic." This is the ministry of the church, rooted in the apostolic message of proclaiming Jesus Christ. This is the "function" of ministry—from the early church to the present.

---

31. P. T. Forsyth, *The Church and the Sacraments*, 3rd ed. (London: Independent, 1949 [1917]), 139.

This means, said Forsyth, that "the Apostolic succession is the Evangelical succession. Its continuity lies not in a due devolution but in a common inspiration, a common ministration of God's grace as mercy." "Evangelical succession" means a succession of preaching the evangelical gospel of God's redeeming love made known in Jesus Christ and expressed in the cross of Christ where atonement for human sin and reconciliation of sinners with God was accomplished. The church's mandate is to proclaim the message of the gospel in every age.

The grace of God in Jesus Christ is proclaimed and only the gospel message "validates the ministry which created it" (140). An evangelical succession of ministry is the church's ongoing gift, given by God and not created by human actions.

32

A God Who Knows Us

The main thing, the unique thing, in religion is not a God Whom we know but a God Who knows us. Religion turns not on knowing but on being known.[32]

IN "RELIGION" AND IN our faith, we focus on God. God can be said to be the "object" of our "religious knowledge." The question is, most broadly, how does God as "an object of knowledge" differ from every other object of knowledge?

Forsyth answered these questions by saying that God is "the absolute subject" of our knowledge. God is "not something that we approach, with the initiative on our side." Instead, God "takes the initiative and approaches us." So our knowledge of God is the result of God's "revelation."

This is significant because it means that we "find" God because God "first finds us." "That is to say," continued Forsyth, that *"the main thing, the unique thing, in religion is not a God Whom we know but a God Who knows us. Religion turns not on knowing but on being known."*

Realizing this about Christian faith sets our faith apart. We have "a God who knows us." We do not climb a ladder into heaven, pull back the clouds, and look into God's face! Instead, God has descended and come to earth, participating in our human existence in God's Son: Jesus Christ. This is why Christian faith, and

---

32. P. T. Forsyth, *The Principle of Authority in Relation to Certainty, Sanctity and Society* (London: Independent, 1913; 2nd ed. 1952), 148–49.

Forsyth, proclaim that God's revelation came in a person who comes to us, instead of our trying to come to him. We find God in Christ because we—humanity and each of us—have first been found by God. This is the astounding news of the Christian gospel! God takes the initiative, God "makes the first move" and comes to us and knows us. Truly, our faith "turns not on knowing but on being known."

33
Living Hope from Christ's Resurrection

> In Christ God not only comes near to us but by an eternal act makes us His own. We hold for ever only because here we are seized and held by the eternal. God *has*, by the resurrection of Christ, regenerated us into a living hope; He has not simply given us a living hope that we may one day be regenerate (1 Pet 1:3). Any living hope we have is the action of Christ's resurrection in us.[33]

WHEN WE USE THE word "hope" we usually think of something we trust will happen in the future. I "hope" for this . . . or that. As we express it now, hope is "to come." But Christian hope is a certainty which we can believe and experience here and now!

Christian hope comes from God and is grounded in Jesus Christ. Hope comes to believers because we are held by God. As Forsyth wrote: "In Christ God not only comes near to us but by an eternal act makes us His own. We hold for ever only because here we are seized and held by the eternal." This is who we are—united by faith with God in Jesus Christ and held by God in Christ.

For us, "God *has*, by the resurrection of Christ, regenerated us into a living hope; He has not simply given us a living hope that we may one day be regenerate (1 Pet 1:3). Any living hope we have is the action of Christ's resurrection in us." Forsyth was interpreting 1 Pet 1:3: "By his great mercy he has given us a new birth into

---

33. P. T. Forsyth, *The Person and Place of Jesus Christ* (London: Independent, 1909; rpt. 1955), 57.

67

a living hope through the resurrection of Jesus Christ from the dead." Our hope is grounded in Christ's resurrection. It is a hope that is present in us and with us in the here and now. We belong to God (are "regenerate") in Jesus Christ. Christ's resurrection is active in us, assuring us of eternal hope, in the lives we live today. This is the power of Christ's resurrection!

34
A Sacrament Does Something

> A Sacrament is as much more than a symbol as a symbol is more than a memorial. It is quite inadequate to speak of the sacrament as an object-lesson—as if its purpose were to convey new truth instead of the living Redeemer.[34]

THE CHURCH LIVES BY the Word and Sacrament. Protestant churches, and the Reformed theological tradition of which P. T. Forsyth was a part, have believed in two sacraments: Baptism and the Lord's Supper. While there is a difference in what each sacrament means, they both share the characteristics of a sacrament, according to the church.

Yet there have also been differences among Protestant churches (and Reformed churches) about the nature of a sacrament and whether a sacrament *conveys* God's grace; or whether a sacrament is a symbol that helps us *remember* God's grace.

Forsyth clearly believed a sacrament *does* something. On the Lord's Supper, he dismissed the idea that the act is "mainly commemorative." He said, "How can we have a mere memorial of one who is still alive, still our life, still present with us and acting in us?" There is "God's action as the cause within our act." A sacrament is not an "object-lesson—as if its purpose were to convey new truth instead of the living Redeemer."

---

34. P. T. Forsyth, *The Church and the Sacraments*, 3rd ed. (London: Independent, 1949 [1917]), 228–29.

Continuing, Forsyth believed that in the "older sense" of symbol: "the symbol contains and conveys the significate, and is a really sacramental thing." This meant, he said, that "Christ offers anew to us, as He did at the Supper, the finished offering which on the Cross He gave to God once for all" (229). The sacraments are "the Word, the Gospel itself, visible, as in preaching the Word is audible." As an act, a sacrament is "Christ in a real presence giving us anew His Redemption" (176). A sacrament is "an act in which he intends to convey *himself*, his mind, his will, his act" (176).

35

The Purpose of the World

> The purpose of a world created by a holy God must be holiness, the reflection and communion of His own holiness.[35]

WHEN WE THINK OF God, we may think of the power of God. By this is often meant God's almighty power to do anything God wants. This is sometimes called "omnipotence."

But theologians stress that God's omnipotence means God's ability to do all things that do not conflict with the divine will or nature. God will not act against who God is.

Put positively, Forsyth wrote that God "can do only the things that are congruous with His moral, His holy nature and purpose." He believed holiness was God's very essence. When it comes to creation, and especially the creation of the world, this meant for Forsyth that "the purpose of a world created by a holy God must be holiness, the reflection and communion of His own holiness." God's nature permeates the world God created. The world must reflect God's holiness; and exist in a relationship of communion with its holy creator.

Can God do this? Does God have the power to carry out this purpose in a world riddled by sin? Can God overcome un-holiness or sin in the world for it to carry out a "holy destiny"? Forsyth said this was "the ultimate question in life."

---

35. P. T. Forsyth, *The Person and Place of Jesus Christ* (London: Independent, 1909; rpt. 1955), 228.

Forsyth believed "Christ and His cross are the answer" to this question. The "omnipotence of holiness" is "to subdue all natural powers and forces, all natural omnipotence, to the moral sanctity of the Kingdom of God." Christ in his cross "surmounts all principalities and powers, things past and present, and to come, every other omnipotence . . . in the Holy One of God, who by His cross is the same world-conqueror yesterday, to-day, and for ever" (229; see Rom 8:38–39).

The purpose of the world will ultimately be carried out. In fact, Forsyth suggests, "God "has it already done in the hollow of His hand" (229).

36

The Greatest Function of the Church

> The greatest function of the Church in full communion with Him is priestly. It is to confess, to sacrifice, to intercede for the whole human race in Him.[36]

THE CHURCH DOES MANY things. Its various actions and activities cover a range of focuses. The church concentrates on the life and needs of its church members. It also looks beyond itself to the world and to ways the church can serve those in need in any place or context throughout the world.

Forsyth maintained the church exercises a "collective priesthood." He saw New Testament Christianity as "a priestly religion or it is nothing. It gathers about a priestly cross on earth and a Great High Priest Eternal in the heavens," Jesus Christ (see Heb 4:14).

If so, Forsyth believed "the greatest function of the Church in full communion with Him is priestly. It is to confess, to sacrifice, to intercede for the whole human race in Him." This is a very comprehensive ministry! The church is to carry out a priest's function: to represent the people before God.

The people are the "whole human race." The church confesses the sins of all humanity before God. The church sacrifices for all others—as did Jesus Christ who "loved us and gave himself up for us" (Eph 5:2). The church intercedes on behalf of the whole human

---

36. P. T. Forsyth, *The Person and Place of Jesus Christ* (London: Independent, 1909; rpt. 1955), 12.

race, praying for them to God, even as Jesus Christ and the Holy Spirit carry out this ministry (see Rom 8:26–34). The church cares about the sins of the world and as a priestly people appeals to God on behalf of the whole human race.

The church can declare to the world that forgiveness of sins is found in Jesus Christ as penitential people confess their sins and find "absolution and remission of its sins in Him." This is the church's message on which it stands and which it proclaims. The church is weighted down by the sins of the world. But the church has "the word of the atoning cross for the lifting of it."

37
In Christ Jesus by Faith

> To be perfect is to be in Christ Jesus by faith. It is the right relation to God in Christ, not the complete achievement of Christian character.[37]

THERE HAS BEEN A strand in Christian theology and devotion that emphasizes the Christian life's aim is to achieve "perfection." Jesus' words: "Be perfect, therefore, as your heavenly Father is perfect" (Matt 5:48) have been seen as an impetus for Christians to seek to attain a growth in faith where full obedience can bring a full or complete Christian sanctification. Some see this as a state of perfect love, or perfect righteousness and true holiness which may be attained by every Christian believer.

But Forsyth maintained "perfection" is not of conduct, but of faith. Faith is the "obedience of the soul" which is "the saving power and perfection for all." "To be perfect is to be in Christ Jesus by faith," said Forsyth. For "it is the right relation to God in Christ, not the complete achievement of Christian character." Faith is a completeness of trust; and it is this faith which gives us the righteousness of God (Rom 1:17).

Christians grow in faith and holiness. This is the work of the Holy Spirit within us. But our salvation does not depend on perfect adherence to the law of God or doing "good works" or anything we can do on our own.

37. P. T. Forsyth, *Christian Perfection* (London: Hodder & Stoughton, 1899), 62.

"In faith we are in the right and perfect relation to God," said Forsyth (63). Faith is the gift of God and our growth in faith is by the work of the Holy Spirit who dwells within us and abides with us (John 14:17; Rom 8:9). The Spirit's work is God's gift of grace to those who believe in Jesus. For "in giving Christ He gave us all things—i.e. perfection," said Forsyth. Our "perfection" is not sinlessness; it in faith—the gift of God.

38

Finished Reconciliation

> The finished reconciliation, the setting up of the New Covenant by Christ, meant that human guilt was once for all robbed of its power to prevent the consummation of the Kingdom of God.[38]

FORSYTH TOOK SERIOUSLY THE New Testament descriptions of the atoning death of Jesus Christ providing the reconciliation of the world to God in Christ (2 Cor. 5:16–21). For Forsyth, Christ's death was very much a "finished reconciliation": "Reconciliation is final in *Jesus Christ and His Cross*, done once for all" (77). This means "in history the great victory is not still to be won; it has been won in reality, and has only to be followed up and secured in actuality. In the spiritual place, in Christ Jesus, in the divine nature, the victory has been won" (77). This is the world-changing and life-changing reality.

Implications of the finished reconciliation of God and humanity through Christ are far-reaching. Among a number of meanings that emerge from this theological conviction is Forsyth's saying that "the finished reconciliation, the setting up of the New Covenant by Christ, meant that human guilt was once for all robbed of its power to prevent the consummation of the Kingdom of God." The power of guilt has been broken in the world. Sin has been defeated. But along with sin against God is guilt before God.

---

38. P. T. Forsyth, *The Work of Christ* (London: Hodder & Stoughton, 1910), 78.

For God is a holy God and human sinners stand guilty before God's holiness. This expressed Forsyth's conviction that "everything begins and ends in our Christian theology with the holiness of God" (78). For "it is the holiness of God which makes sin guilt. It is the holiness of God that necessitates the work of Christ, that calls for it, and that provides it" (79).

Jesus Christ's finished work of reconciliation has defeated and disarmed the power of guilt for those who stand before the holy God. Christ changes our relationship with God, now and forever. Sin is forgiven; guilt is gone. In Christ, "everything has become new!" (2 Cor 5:17).

39

Christ Redeemed the Human Race

> It was the race that Christ redeemed, and not a mere bouquet of believers. It was a Church He saved, and not a certain pale of souls. Each soul is saved in a universal and corporate salvation.[39]

FORSYTH'S VIEWS ABOUT THE future—and of future salvation—have been debated by scholars who study Forsyth. Some believe Forsyth embraces universalism—the view that all persons will be saved. Others reject this reading of Forsyth. Some have called Forsyth's views a "hopeful universalism."

The view that all persons will be saved has always had a place in the history of theology but it has never been the "majority report" among theologians, or with Christian churches. Forsyth spoke of Christ redeeming the human race—and not just part of it. He wrote: "It was the race that Christ redeemed, and not a mere bouquet of believers. It was a Church He saved, and not a certain pale of souls." In this, he stood in line with various early church theologians such as Origen. Other contemporaries of Forsyth also wrote along these lines as did (later), Karl Barth. But Forsyth did not openly embrace a dogma of "universal salvation."

Forsyth looked toward the sanctification of all things by God's holy love. He believed that through Christ's cross and resurrection, the power of death has been broken—once and for all. This means

---

39. P. T. Forsyth, *The Church and the Sacraments*, 3rd ed. (London: Independent, 1949 [1917]), 43.

death is not the determinative power for human destiny. Jesus Christ is victor! Salvation comes through Christ's incarnation, atonement, and resurrection by the work of the Holy Spirit—not through any human will or power. God's holy determination is to bring those for whom Christ died—to respond to Christ—and realize salvation: "The object of the Gospel is no longer to save a group out of the world, but to save the world itself" (125). For Forsyth, if it is possible for the whole world to be saved—should we not desire this to be so?!

40

Christ Is Savior of the World

> This is just what each man is entitled through Christ to say. "I am chosen and elect of God." There is no man who has not a right to say that with Christ's Cross for his charter. The sin of unfaith is refusing to say it, *i.e.* refusing Christ and the God Christ brings. For that God is the Saviour of a world which has its concrete existence only in its souls. He is the Saviour of such a race, and not a section of it. In the Cross Christ became absolutely final, and universal, and particular. That is what faith says, and what it ensues.[40]

FORSYTH'S VIEW OF THE cross of Christ was that Christ's death was universal in scope. That is, in Christ, all persons can claim their election and chosenness by God since Christ died for all. Forsyth wrote that each person "is entitled through Christ to say. 'I am chosen and elect of God.'" Forsyth went on to say that our election is to "a priority of service" (360). We are saved *to serve* God and others. This is our obedience to the God who saves in Jesus Christ.

Faith is the "personal receptivity" to believing in Christ, "the response to it" (356). "The sin of unfaith," said Forsyth, is "refusing to say it, *i.e.* refusing Christ and the God Christ brings." Christ is the "Saviour of a world" (John 3:16), a savior of "such a race, and not a section of it," the "salvation of a world of souls, a new

---

40. P. T. Forsyth, *The Principle of Authority in Relation to Certainty, Sanctity and Society* (London: Independent, 1913; 2nd ed. 1952), 354–55.

Humanity" (355). The "lost," said Forsyth, are "lost by refusing that Gospel in their mysterious and incalculable freedom" (357).

This meant for Forsyth that "the certainty of revelation and faith is that in the universal Christ the world is chosen for salvation, and is saved in principle, and shall be saved in fact" (357). The world is redeemed by God in Christ and God's work—the kingdom of God—is set up and is a reality!

41

God's Holy Love Is Omnipotent for Ever

> The Gospel is not just a message that God is love; but it is the historic act in which God's holy love is installed as omnipotent for ever among the world's powers and affairs. It is not the cheery word of a great good comrade . . . but the decisive power and action of the royal omnipotent, absolute Master of every fate, the last victorious Reality of history, with Whom we have for ever to do, and to Whom for ever we belong and we turn.[41]

GOD'S HOLY LOVE WAS enacted in the cross of Jesus Christ. This is the decisive event in history. Now, wrote Forsyth, "God's holy love is installed as omnipotent for ever among the world's powers and affairs." The destiny of history is secured. The gospel message is that God's holy love is the dominant power among all other powers on earth—now and forever. All expressions of human power—social, cultural, or political—bow before the ultimate power of God's holy love expressed in the cross of Jesus Christ. Redemption, reconciliation, and the kingdom of God are realities.

God as Lord of all (Acts 10:36) has acted, decisively in Christ. This is the "last reality of the world." God's "historic holiness" is "the power fundamental, and at last irresistible in all cosmic things, as their last authority, therefore, and their final wealth and

---

41. P. T. Forsyth, "Religion and Reality," *The Contemporary Review* 115 (1919) 551–52.

fullness" (551) This expresses Isaiah's temple vision: "'Holy, holy, holy is the Lord of hosts; the whole earth is full of his glory'" (Isa 6:3). God's holiness is the last reality.

The triumph of God's holy love as "omnipotent for ever" is "the last victorious Reality of history," said Forsyth. Forever, we have to do with this God of holy love. God's holy love has vanquished the evil world. Evil has no future. It is overcome in Christ. Creation will be sanctified. Universal holiness will be established. Individually, corporately, and cosmically, God's holy love is omnipotent. It is to this God "to Whom for ever we belong" (552)!

42

Heaven Laughs Last

> But in Christ's moral, historic, final Cross alone do we learn to interpret the irony of history as the irony of Providence, the tender, portentous smile of a victorious, patient God. If His words are acts, so is that slow smile. Heaven does not laugh loud but it laughs last—when all the world will laugh in its light. It is a smile more immeasurable than ocean's and more deep; it is an irony gentler and more patient than the bending skies, the irony of a long love and the play of its sure mastery; it is the smile of the holy in its silent omnipotence of mercy.[42]

CHRISTIANS ALWAYS ANTICIPATE THE future. Like everyone, we wonder what the ultimate end of history will be like; and what is in store. Unlike others, however, Christians live from the conviction that however history turns out, God will be victorious, accomplishing the divine purpose and that God will "be all in all" (1 Cor 15:28). Whatever else may be said, we believe: "The kingdom of the world has become the kingdom of our Lord and of his Messiah, and he will reign forever and ever" (Rev 11:15).

Forsyth provides a poetic passage (above) fastening the triumph of the "victorious, patient God" to the cross of Jesus Christ alone. "The irony of history" becomes also "the irony of Providence" as God's "tender, portentous" and "slow" smile leads to

---

42. P. T. Forsyth, *The Justification of God* (New York: Charles Scribner's Sons, 1917), 215.

heaven's laugh: "Heaven does not laugh loud but it laughs last—when all the world will laugh in its light."

God has the last word. History belongs to the purposes and providence of God. Jesus Christ, who on his cross appeared to be weak and defeated is, instead, the final victor who has overcome all that would defeat God's holy love, which Jesus embodied. God's "silent omnipotence of mercy" is ultimate and everlasting. Heaven laughs last!

LIVING AS A CHRISTIAN

43
The Organized Hallelujah

> Our chief praise is thanksgiving for the Gospel. And our prayer is Christian only in the name of the Gospel. Preaching is "the organized Hallelujah of an ordered community."[1]

SERVICES OF WORSHIP IN Protestant churches are marked by different "rubrics" or parts. Three key elements of worship are the Praise of God, especially as expressed in hymns and music; Thanksgiving to God, as especially as expressed in prayer; and Preaching in which the gospel message is proclaimed to the gathered community of the church.

Forsyth stressed the importance of preaching as a dimension of worship. Preaching, he believed was "the great, common, universal faith addressing the faith of the local community" (94). The preacher "reflects the faith of the great true Church" (94). For "nothing in the service goes to the root of the Gospel (and, therefore, of the Church) like preaching."

Then Forsyth went on to say, "Our chief praise is thanksgiving for the Gospel. And our prayer is Christian only in the name of the Gospel. Preaching is 'the organized Hallelujah of an ordered community.'" We praise and thank God for the gospel of Jesus Christ. When we pray we do so in the name of Jesus Christ, who is himself the gospel.

---

1. P. T. Forsyth, *Positive Preaching and Modern Mind* (London: Hodder & Stoughton, 1907; rpt. 1981), 95.

Preaching as "the organized Hallelujah" of the Christian community enables us to hear the gospel proclaimed to us through preaching. Preaching in the church enables worship to happen as the people of God hear the Word of God proclaimed and respond to the gospel through the different dimensions of worship. Preaching stirs hearers to worship—to the praise and joy of God: Hallelujah! Preaching leads to prayer in thanks to God. Preaching enables worshipers to engage the gospel message in what they say and do!

44
Daily Cleansings of Channels of Grace

> Every believer has more or less of this sin in him, and the risk of it always. But it does not cut him off from the divine life. There is a daily confession, a daily forgiveness, a daily cleansing of the channels of the grace of God.[2]

WHEN OVENS WITH TIMERS were being introduced, their advertising slogan was: "Set it and forget it." Even if the preacher preached overtime, the Sunday dinner roast would not be ruined because the timer would ensure it would not cook too long. Set it and forget it!

Some people have the "set it and forget it" view of the Christian life. Once they have been "saved," they believe they can set their lives on "automatic pilot" and have no need to worry about sin.

But Christian believers still sin. We still break God's laws, fall short of God's glory, and do not always live as God desires. Forsyth points out that while "every believer has more or less of this sin in him, and the risk of it always," this does not cut us off "from the divine life. There is a daily confession, a daily forgiveness, a daily cleansing of the channels of the grace of God."

This is a word to encourage us. God gives us means by which our sin can be forgiven: by confession and seeking forgiveness. Daily we confess and seek God's forgiveness. There is a "daily

---

2. P. T. Forsyth, *Christian Perfection* (London: Hodder & Stoughton, 1899), 22.

cleansing of the channels of the grace of God" as we use the means God gives us by which God's grace may be received. These can include Scripture reading, prayer, the fellowship of other Christians, and reconciliation with those whom we have hurt or wronged. Through these, we will not be cut off from life lived in a relationship of trust and love of God.

We cannot take our Christian lives for granted; or think sin does not matter. Day by day we use "the channels of the grace of God" in confession and forgiveness to receive anew the grace of God which blesses us.

45
The Greatest Benefit in Life

> It is the goodness of God, His holy love, as it sinks in, that brings home to us what Schiller teaches, that "the greatest bane of life is guilt"; because it makes us first know and feel that the greatest boon of life is grace. Only the good know how bad they were.[3]

IT TAKES TIME FOR us to experience the goodness of God. It takes time for us to experience God's holy love. As we live as Christians, experiencing life day by day, if we are sensitive and aware, we will know ways in which God's goodness becomes real to us. We will recognize God's holy love time and time again when we find the strength and comfort we need.

But as we experience God's goodness and holy love, we will also become aware of our sinfulness and guilt when we live apart from God. The contrast between who God is and who we are is dramatic and can be disheartening. This is why Forsyth noted that "it is the goodness of God, His holy love, as it sinks in, that brings home to us what Schiller teaches, that 'the greatest bane of life is guilt.' As we know more and more who God is; we realize more and more how we "fall short of the glory of God" (Rom 3:23). No wonder Forsyth quotes Schiller as saying the greatest bane (misery) in life is guilt!

---

3. P. T. Forsyth, "The Goodness of God" (1911) in *Revelation Old and New: Sermons and Addresses*, ed. John Huxtable (London: Independent, 1962), 83.

However. As we look at ourselves and see guilt, we also look at God's goodness and holy love. When we do, we "first know and feel that the greatest boon (benefit) in life is grace." God's grace is greater than our sin. God's goodness and holy love finds us by grace and blesses us. This is the greatest benefit in life. We can imagine nothing greater and more wonderful than experiencing God's boundless goodness and God's holy love, which forgives our sin through Jesus Christ and which brings us faith.

46
Trust the Bad to the Merciful God

> All we can do with the bad is what we must do with our own souls—commit and trust it to God, and to the merciful God, the God of a final, consummate, and holy salvation.[4]

THERE IS BAD IN life. "Bad" comes in many forms. We recognize it on the big scale of human history as well as in the daily lives we live.

The "biggest bad" may be the mystery of evil. We cannot explain why evil exists. Evil is that which is contrary to God. It is that which is "against God." In the Bible, evil is connected to sin. When sin enters, evil appears. Where humans are concerned, where they use their freedom without regard to God—evil or the "bad" occurs. As far back as the story of Noah we read: "The LORD saw that the wickedness of humankind was great in the earth, and that every inclination of the thoughts of their hearts was only evil continually" (Gen 6:5). Forsyth referred to the "causation of the bad" as "the mystery of human freedom."

But the bad is within us, as well. We sin. We act against God. We offend against God's holy love for us. We cannot explain why we choose to act in these ways. All we can do is confess our sin.

So Forsyth said, "All we can do with the bad is what we must do with our own souls—commit and trust it to God, and to the

---

4. P. T. Forsyth, *The Principle of Authority in Relation to Certainty, Sanctity and Society* (London: Independent, 1913; 2nd ed. 1952), 357.

merciful God, the God of a final, consummate, and holy salvation." In confessing sin, we entrust ourselves to the merciful God. Only God can forgive and reconcile us, in Jesus Christ. Only the merciful God can bring us to final salvation. We entrust the wicked—and we ourselves—to the God of mercy and holy love. We trust the bad to the merciful God, who will absorb all the "bad" and "evil" in carrying out the divine purposes of supreme salvation in Jesus Christ—now and forever!

47
A Living Piety

> Christian life which does not grow out of Christian doctrine becomes a failure. . . . You cannot keep Christian piety alive except upon Christian truth.[5]

SOME HAVE SAID CHRISTIANITY is like a coin: it has two sides. One dimension of Christian faith is our beliefs, the theological understandings we believe to be true. This is not left solely up to us. The Christian church, through the centuries, has wrestled with what Christians believe. Early creeds such as the Nicene and Apostles' Creed indicate ways early Christian beliefs were formulated.

For others, Christianity is primary about a way of living—the other side of the Christian "coin." How shall we live as disciples of Jesus Christ, those who have responded to his command: "Follow me" (Mark 2:14)? Faithful Christian action is the main focus—for Christian churches and Christian lives.

Forsyth maintained that "doctrine and life are really two sides of one Christianity; and they are equally indispensable, because Christianity is living truth. It is not merely truth; it is not simply life. It is living truth" (43). This is the fullness of Christianity and Christian faith.

To live the truth, we must know the truth. This meant for Forsyth that "Christian life which does not grow out of Christian doctrine becomes a failure." The church's life—and our lives—must

---

5. P. T. Forsyth, *The Work of Christ* (London: Hodder & Stoughton, 1910), 44.

grow and be nurtured by the church's faith and our faith. Christian life lives from Christian belief. Said Forsyth: "You cannot keep Christian piety alive except upon Christian truth."

The challenge for us is to understand our faith—what the church believes and what we believe and to enact our belief in our lives as disciples of Jesus Christ and members of the body of Christ, the church. Our Christian piety lives from our beliefs. So Forsyth wrote that "it is of supreme importance that we should know what the Christian doctrine is on the great matters." This is the way our Christian beliefs and Christian lives can be "living truth," a living piety!

48

Where Is Your Heart?

> The question is, What is your home to which your heart returns, either in repentance or in joy? Where is your heart? What is the bent of your will on the whole, the direction and service of your total life?[6]

OUR DAILY LIVES AS Christians are a "mixed bag." We serve God in Christ and others. But we also sin. We are, as Luther had put it, both "justified" and a "sinner."

Sometimes our spells of sin can be frequent or prolonged. We sin, experience guilt; and then ask for God's mercy and forgiveness. We repent and vow to live better in the service of our Master.

Forsyth addressed this by saying that we may stay in a house, then leave the house occasionally—for good or for ill. But the ultimate question is: "What is your home to which your heart returns, either in repentance or in joy? Where is your heart? What is the bent of your will on the whole, the direction and service of your total life?"

We have to ask ourselves the deepest question of where our true home is—in faith with God; or in following our own pursuits and passion? Where is your heart?

Over the course of your life, what is the "bent of your will on the whole?" Have you sought self or service? Have you loved the

---

6. P. T. Forsyth, *Christian Perfection* (London: Hodder & Stoughton, 1899), 34.

things of the world—the "things of the flesh"? Or, have you loved most to set your mind on "the things of the Spirit" (Rom 8:5)?

Put another way, Forsyth asked: "On which side have you stood and striven, under which King have you served or died?" Whom have we served through our life? What is "the direction and service of your total life?"

What matters most is Christ and faith, said Forsyth. Truly, "our prevailing habit of soul and bent of will is Christ's" (43). Our heart belongs to Christ!

49

Faith and Praise

> Faith is for the Christian enveloped in praise.[7]

DID YOU EVER NOTICE Christian worship begins with praise and thanksgiving? A call to worship, a hymn—praise is given to God: Father, Son, and Holy Spirit.

Confession of sin has its place. It is necessary for God's people to confess what they have done . . . and what they have failed to do. The praise of God leads to confession before God, seeking God's forgiveness and blessing. As our sin is forgiven, we again praise God.

Praise expresses faith and, as Forsyth commented, "faith is for the Christian enveloped in praise." Faith is "no gloomy humility, no sombre patience, no dull endurance, no resentful submission. It is all clothed with hope. It is the faith and submission of a soul that knows itself both immortal and redeemed, and owes all to God's purely marvellous grace. Its atmosphere is glad hope."

Christians are people of faith, hope, . . . and praise! Indeed, said Forsyth, "The spirit of Christian life and worship is thanks and praise" (138). This is because faith is focused on Christ and his death for us for the forgiveness of sin and reconciliation with God. Faith is "enveloped in praise" for believers because faith is the "joyful response to our redemption" (138). There is no greater response faith can make than the deepest sense of thanksgiving

---

7. P. T. Forsyth, *Christian Perfection* (London: Hodder & Stoughton, 1899), 137.

and praise to God for the "good news of great joy for all the people" (Luke 2:10). For "God proves his love for us in that while we still were sinners Christ died for us" (Rom 5:8). This is the "glad hope" of faith, which evokes our greatest praise!

Forsyth said that Christian public worship "should open as well as close with a doxology." Faith begins and ends "enveloped in praise." What else can faith do except praise since it "owes all to God's purely marvellous grace!"

50
Believe, Be, and Abide in Christ

> To believe in Christ, to be in Christ, and to abide in Christ, are three stages of the same perfection—which you may call the Petrine, the Pauline, and the Johannine stages if you will.[8]

A BASIC WORD OF Jesus was to his disciples: "If any want to become my followers, let them deny themselves and take up their cross and follow me" (Matt 16:24). Jesus was saying that being his followers meant persons had to relinquish control of their own lives and give control to Jesus. This reminds us of Paul's words: "I have been crucified with Christ; and it is no longer I who live, but it is Christ who lives in me" (Gal 2:19–20). Or, as Forsyth put it, a person is "perfect when he comes to belong to Christ instead of himself."

Forsyth also points out three stages of this belonging to Christ: "To believe in Christ, to be in Christ, and to abide in Christ," which he says, "you may call the Petrine, the Pauline, and the Johannine stages if you will."

Believe, *be*, and *abide* in Christ. These dimensions hearken to New Testament passages: Peter's confession of belief at Caesarea Philippi: "'You are the Messiah, the Son of the living God'" (Matt 16:16); Paul's declaration: "If anyone is in Christ, there is a new creation: everything old has passed away; see, everything has become new!" (2 Cor 5:17); and from the Gospel of John: "Abide in

---

8. P. T. Forsyth, *Christian Perfection* (London: Hodder & Stoughton, 1899), 108.

me as I abide in you" (John 15:4). These move us from confession of believing in Christ, to being a new person who belongs to Christ, to abiding in Christ from now and forever.

Do we see our lives in these perspectives? Is our confession of Christ focused on who Jesus Christ is—the eternal Son of God? Is Christ transforming our lives from self-control to Christ's control so our one desire is to live for Christ? Is your life lived with a lively sense of the presence of Christ with you and your continual abiding in union with Christ?

Believe, be, and *abide* in Christ!

51

Living Communion

> Nothing short of living, loving, holy, habitual communion between His holy soul and ours can realise at last the end which God achieved in Jesus Christ.[9]

THE DEATH OF JESUS Christ on the cross is described as bringing reconciliation: "In Christ God was reconciling the world to himself, not counting their trespasses against them, and entrusting the message of reconciliation to us" (2 Cor 5:19). This action has forever changed the relationship between God and humanity. As Forsyth stated, this is "a change of relation from alienation to communion" (57). In the death of Jesus Christ, humanity has been forgiven for sin. "The human race as one whole" is now reconciled to the holy God, who is its creator and redeemer.

But Forsyth continued to say that reconciliation leads not only to "peace and confidence, but to reciprocal communion." For "the grand end of reconciliation is communion" (57). Communion now marks the relationship between God and forgiven sinners. There is now an ongoing relationship of communion—a union of God and God's people—which marks the lives we live, every day. This is a great result of Christ's death on the cross. For "nothing short of living, loving, holy, habitual communion between His holy soul and ours can realise at last the end which God achieved in Jesus Christ."

---

9. P. T. Forsyth, *The Work of Christ* (London: Hodder & Stoughton, 1910), 58.

The benefits of Christ's reconciliation are many. But the ongoing, continual communion of God in Christ with those reconciled by Christ gives us a relationship of intimacy with God. Our communion frees us to pray to God, to recognize God's communication with us, as well as God's guidance for our lives so we may serve God freely and fully. Christ is our constant companion. Through him, we are in the presence of God as Christ continually intercedes for us (Rom 8:34).

Our "reciprocal communion" means a full relationship with God in Christ. There is shared communion—as we commune and speak with God; and as God communicates and joins with us. We have a living communion with God!

52

A Personal Christ

> Faith in Christ (as a last word) is faith in a Christ personal to us. . . . He must be personal to us. He must be our Saviour, in our situation, our needs, loves, shames, sins. He must not only live but mingle with our lives. . . . That is the Christ we need, and, thank God for His unspeakable gift, that is the Christ we have.[10]

WE READ OF JESUS in the New Testament, particularly in the Gospels. The biblical books tell us of the historic Christ—Jesus of Nazareth, who lived and died and was raised from the dead.

The New Testament also tells us of the early church, of women and men who believed Jesus was alive, that the Holy Spirit of God brought them into Christ's living presence.

But there is a third step. Forsyth spoke of the historic Christ, the living Christ, and then the Christ who is personal to us. All Jesus said and did and was is as the living Christ who is now "for us." As Forsyth put it: "Faith in Christ (as a last word) is faith in a Christ personal to us. . . . He must be personal to us. He must be our Saviour, in our situation, our needs, loves, shames, sins. He must not only live but mingle with our lives." The Christ who is personal to us is not only *"a* savior" or *"the* savior," but also *"my* savior."

---

10. P. T. Forsyth, *God the Holy Father* (London: Independent, 1955), 96. Originally in *The Holy Father and the Living Christ* (1897).

My savior is with me in my situations. He meets my needs, blesses my loves. He takes on my shames, my sins. He is in the midst of my life. Communion with the living Christ in a personal relationship is the reality of my Christian faith.

Thinking of the richness of Jesus Christ led Paul to exclaim, "Thanks be to God for his indescribable gift!" (2 Cor 9:15). The Christ who is in our lives and is active within us as we are united with him by faith is, said Forsyth, "the Christ we need, and, thank God for His unspeakable gift, that is the Christ we have." The personal Christ is "Heart amidst our heart and its ruins and its resurrection!"

53

On Eternal Rock

> That is the certainty and freedom of faith, the certainty that we are objects of the eternal choice before and beneath all the foundations of the world, members of a creation whose ground plan is its movement to the everlasting Redemption, and destined for the kingdom against which no power can prevail. To be settled there is to be on eternal rock.[11]

LIFE IS FILLED WITH uncertainties. It doesn't take us long to recognize this. So many things happen to us that we find our "plans" always need to be revisable since unforeseen circumstances and events frequently call for "mid-course" adjustments!

In the biggest picture, we wonder what we can rely upon? What is a foundation that will not be "shaken" amid all the contingencies we encounter? Is there anything that is stable in an uncertain and changing world?

In faith, we can say, "Yes." There is eternal certainty that stands in the midst of all changes and uncertainties.

Forsyth wrote: "That is the certainty and freedom of faith, the certainty that we are objects of the eternal choice before and beneath all the foundations of the world, members of a creation whose ground plan is its movement to the everlasting Redemption,

---

11. P. T. Forsyth, *The Principle of Authority in Relation to Certainty, Sanctity and Society* (London: Independent, 1913; 2nd ed. 1952), 352.

and destined for the kingdom against which no power can prevail. To be settled there is to be on eternal rock."

These words hearken back to the words of the Psalmist about God: "He alone is my rock and my salvation, my fortress; I shall never be shaken" (Ps 62:2; cf. v. 6). God's eternal choice of us, from the "foundation of the world" (Eph 1:4), to be part of creation, moving to "everlasting Redemption," says Forsyth, assures us that we are "destined for the kingdom against which no power can prevail."

This is the greatest foundation for life imaginable! Nothing can shake the eternal purposes of God at work in the world toward redemption. "To be settled" in this reality is "to be on eternal rock!"

54
Saints

> The saints, in the New Testament, are not the saintly but the believing. What Christ always demanded of those who came to Him was not character, not achievement, but faith, trust. His standard was not conduct, it was not character, it was not creed. It was faith in Himself as God's Grace. It was trust, and trust not in His manner but in His message, His Gospel.[12]

WE ARE USED TO hearing the word "saint" used to describe a unique and virtuous person. Their activities are moral and upright so we hear: "She's a saint."

The term "saint" is used for individuals like this. However, in the New Testament, the word "saint" is always used in the plural. Paul often began his letters by writing to "the saints," such as: "To the saints who are in Ephesus" (Eph 1:1; cf. Phil 1:1).

Thus we find Forsyth saying that New Testament-wise, the saints are "not the saintly but the believing." *All Christians* are saints! So Paul addresses whole church congregations.

It is "not achievement, but faith, trust" which puts us among the company of saints. It is not what we "do," but our faith and trust. Not "character" or "creed," but for Jesus it was "faith in Himself as God's Grace" that mattered and that puts us in the fellowship of the

---

12. P. T. Forsyth, *Christian Perfection* (London: Hodder & Stoughton, 1899), 81.

church, of the saints of God. The focus of faith is Jesus himself, *not us*—our virtues, morality, or achievements.

Faith is trust *in Jesus Christ*. Saints are those who believe and trust in Christ as God's grace in person; and his message, which is the gospel of God (Rom 1:1), made clear to us in his death on the cross for the sin of the world (Rom 5:8).

Saints make up the fellowship of the Christian church. They are sinners who are redeemed by God's grace, with sin forgiven, and reconciliation established with God. Rejoice in the communion of all God's saints!

55
Holy People Don't Feel They Are Holy

> The holiest have ever been so because they dared not feel they were. Their sanctity grew unconsciously from their worship of His.[13]

THERE'S AN IRONIC SAYING, quoting someone as saying: "Last year, I was conceited. This year, I am perfect!" We smile since we know thinking one is "perfect" goes against all reality and is the height of conceit!

The same is true with "holiness." In Christian spirituality, devotion and purity of life is a mark of Christian discipleship. These witness to the work of the Holy Spirit. The Spirit initiates and sustains growth in faith, helping Christians avoid sin and live in accordance with God's will. This is our "holiness," in being set apart for God's purposes, growing in faith, and obeying God's desires in all things.

Christians never attain perfection! Paradoxically, the more we think we are "holy," the "less holy" we are. As Forsyth noted, "The height of sinlessness means the deepest sense of sin." We are the "most holy" when we recognize we are the "least holy." Holiness can never be our conceit; and we must say: "Christ Jesus came into the world to save sinners—of whom I am the foremost" (1 Tim 1:15).

---

13. P. T. Forsyth, *Christian Perfection* (London: Hodder & Stoughton, 1899), 10.

Thus, as Forsyth said, "The holiest have ever been so because they dared not feel they were. Their sanctity grew unconsciously from their worship of His." Considering God's holiness shows us how impossible it is for us to be "holy" in ourselves. It is only God's Spirit within us, recognized and received by faith, that works for "holiness" within our lives—the ongoing growth in faith and living in obedience to God in all things. We ourselves can never, ever, claim any credit for being "holy." It is all the work and gift of the Spirit. This is why we can note that holy people do not feel they are holy. In worshiping the holy God, we see ourselves as sinners, even as we are people who are saved by faith in the atoning death of Jesus Christ. We are Christians, but still sinners in need of daily forgiveness. Our praise and thanks is to God who forgives—even "unholy" people!

56

Sin Which Stays and Sin Which Visits

> There is sin as the principle of a soul and sin as an incident, sin which stays and sin which visits. Visitations of sin may cleave indefinitely to the new life, and the freedom to sin and the risk are always there. The great justification does not dispense with the daily forgiveness.[14]

SIN IS PART OF our daily lives as Christians. We believe the ultimate power of sin is broken by Jesus Christ for us, yet we still sin, and we must still ask for God's forgiveness.

In Forsyth's terms, there is a difference between sin as a principle of life—the way one lives; and sin that occurs at various times in our (Christian) experience. Forsyth wrote: "There is sin as the principle of a soul and sin as an incident" or: "sin which stays and sin which visits." Is sin a *point* along your life-line; or does it *define* your life-line itself?

For "visitations of sin may cleave indefinitely to the new life, and the freedom to sin and the risk are always there." Christians are realists about sin. We know we are constantly in need of forgiveness. This is the story of our Christian lives. There is what Hebrews calls "the sin that clings so closely" (Heb 12:1).

Forsyth points out that "the great justification does not dispense with the daily forgiveness." We are justified by faith in Christ (Rom 5:1), but we are sinners still. Yet the difference between sin

---

14. P. T. Forsyth, *Christian Perfection* (London: Hodder & Stoughton, 1899), 45.

which stays and sin which visits is that as Christians we do seek daily forgiveness from God. As a bumper sticker put it: "Christians are not perfect; just forgiven." We need daily forgiveness. As Forsyth continued, "There is the great forgiveness from sin which we ask in Christ's name alone, and there is its detail in the daily forgiveness which depends also on our forgiving daily." God forgives us; and we are to forgive others. As Paul wrote, we are to be "forgiving one another, as God in Christ has forgiven you" (Eph 4:32). May sin be only our "visitor."

57
Speaking with God

> Every form of prayer is speech with God the Father and Redeemer. "Praise is the speech of faith, petition is the speech of hope, intercession is the speech of love, confession is the speech of repentance."[15]

PRAYER IS CENTRAL TO our Christian lives. It is the heartbeat of our faith. Forsyth called prayer "a habit, joy, and prize of life" (138). In prayer, "humility takes the form of reverence and yet communion. The heart converses with God in Christ." This is the blessing and joy of prayer!

Forsyth went on to say that prayer is "the inmost energy of faith." Our faith pours itself out in prayer. Prayer is "faith's habit of the heart." Prayer is faith expressed in words. For Forsyth, "Every form of prayer is speech with God the Father and Redeemer. 'Praise is the speech of faith, petition is the speech of hope, intercession is the speech of love, confession is the speech of repentance.'"

The fullness of our Christian faith is expressed in prayer as we speak to God through Jesus Christ. Faith expresses "the praise of [God's] glorious grace that he freely bestowed on us in the Beloved, Jesus Christ" (Eph 1:6). Faith receives God's gift in Christ and praises God's grace through prayer. Our hope in Christ is expressed in words of petition as we speak to God of the deep desires and yearnings of our hearts. We pray for others, in intercession,

---

15. P. T. Forsyth, *Christian Perfection* (London: Hodder & Stoughton, 1899), 139.

in words of love for them, as we commend them and their needs to God, through our advocate, Jesus Christ (1 John 2:1). We confess our sins through the speech of repentance as we seek God's forgiveness for our sins and violation of God's holy love for us in Christ.

In prayer, we have communion with God in Christ. We are given the greatest and deepest blessing imaginable: to converse with God in Christ. Faith's energy bursts forth in prayer as we praise, hope, intercede, and confess. Our human language is heard by God when we convey all that is deep within us as we speak with God!

58
We Live . . . to Pray

> But at last it is truer to say that we live the Christian life in order to pray than that we pray in order to live the Christian life. It is at least as true. Our prayer prepares for our work and sacrifice, but all our work and sacrifice still more prepare for prayer.[16]

WHAT IF OUR WHOLE life as Christians was oriented around prayer? What if we were to take seriously Paul's command: "Pray without ceasing" (1 Thess 5:17)?

Forsyth believed "the Christian life is prayer without ceasing" (86). How is this possible?

Forsyth said, "Prayer is often represented as the great means of the Christian life. But it is no mere means, it is the great end of that life." (17). In other words, prayer is not just the *means* God gives us to help us live as Christians. But prayer itself is *our whole purpose for living* as Christians!

He put it this way: "It is truer to say that we live the Christian life in order to pray than that we pray in order to live the Christian life. It is at least as true. Our prayer prepares for our work and sacrifice, but all our work and sacrifice still more prepare for prayer."

This can reorient us. Our purpose—"the great end" of our lives—is to pray, to converse with God in Jesus Christ. This is our reason for being. Prayer prepares us for Christian living, our life

---

16. P. T. Forsyth, *The Soul of Prayer* (London: Charles H. Kelly, 1916), 18. [2002 ed.—15]

of work and service to God in Christ. We are to "do everything for the glory of God" (1 Cor 10:31). Prayer prepares us to live our discipleship in the world. But, even more, for Forsyth: our continuing discipleship and service prepare us . . . for prayer! We do everything for the glory of God and all we do—prepares us to pray! Our communion with God in prayer is so important that our whole lives, in all their facets—prepare us for prayer with God. We "pray without ceasing"—in what we do; and in our prayers themselves. We live . . . to pray!

59

The Highest Dependence on God

> Faith is the very highest form of our dependence on God. We never outgrow it. We refine it, but we never transcend it. Whatever other fruits of the Spirit we show, they grow upon faith, and faith which is in its nature repentance. Penitence, faith, sanctification, always coexist; they do not destroy and succeed each other; they are phases of the one process of God in the one soul.[17]

WHAT IS FAITH?

We know faith is what we believe. But it is more than intellectual convictions. Faith also involves our will and our emotions. Christian faith envelopes the whole of who we are as persons.

Martin Luther often stressed faith as trust. Faith means our entrusting ourselves to God in Jesus Christ; our depending on God—through thick and thin. Faith is a daring confidence in God.

Forsyth emphasized this conviction when he wrote that "faith is the very highest form of our dependence on God. We never outgrow it. We refine it, but we never transcend it. Whatever other fruits of the Spirit we show, they grow upon faith, and faith which is in its nature repentance." Faith is central and key for us. We trust God in Jesus Christ: "For I know the one in whom I have put my trust" (2 Tim 1:12).

---

17. P. T. Forsyth, *Christian Perfection* (London: Hodder & Stoughton, 1899), 8.

Faith is the means of our salvation in Christ (Rom 4:5). It is pure trust, pure dependence on God—a dependence that marks all our days. We never "outgrow" faith. All we are and do in our Christian lives emerges from faith. Faith expresses itself in repentance, as we confess our sin to God and depend on God's forgiveness in Christ to bind us in communion with God. Forsyth notes that "penitence, faith, sanctification, always coexist; they do not destroy and succeed each other; they are phases of the one process of God in the one soul."

Faith is our highest dependence on God!

60
Ask for Everything in Christ's Name

> Ask for everything you can ask in Christ's name, i.e. everything desirable by a man who is in Christ's kingdom of God, by a man who lives for it at heart, everything in tune with the purpose and work of the kingdom in Christ. If you are in that kingdom, then pray freely for whatever you need or wish to keep you active and effective for it, from daily bread upwards and outwards. In all things make your requests known.[18]

ARE WE TIMID WITH our prayers? Are we sometimes reticent or even afraid to bring some requests to God in prayer?

Forsyth urged: "Do not be so timid about praying wrongly if you pray humbly. If God is really the Father that Christ revealed, then the principle is—take everything to Him that exercises you . . . ." Forsyth said, "apart from frivolity"—like praying to find your lost knife or umbrella—"there is really no limitation in the New Testament on the contents of petitions" (97).

For when we "keep close to the New Testament Christ," we can "ask in Christ's name, i.e. everything desirable." We do this since we are persons of God's kingdom, who "live for it at heart," seeking to be "in tune with the purpose and work of the kingdom in Christ." When this is who we are, we can "pray freely for whatever you need or wish to keep you active and effective for it, from

---

18. P. T. Forsyth, *The Soul of Prayer* (London: Charles H. Kelly, 1916), 97. [2002 ed.—76.]

daily bread upwards and outwards." In this, we follow Paul: "Let your requests be made known to God" (Phil 4:6). We can pray boldly, asking for everything in Christ's name.

What if God does not grant our requests? Forsyth said: "It will not unhinge such faith if you do not obtain them. At least you have laid them on God's heart; and faith means confidences between you and not only favours." We pray confidently to God, knowing that if God does not answer the way we desire, we can trust God's will and purposes.

Ask for everything in Christ's name!

61

Obedient Acceptance

> We can offer God nothing so great and effective as our obedient acceptance of the mind and purpose and work of Christ.... It is a power that grows by exercise. At first it groans, at last it glides.[19]

OUR GREAT ATTITUDE IN prayer should be what Jesus taught us in the Lord's Prayer: "Thy will be done, on earth as it is in heaven" (see Matt 6:10). We want our prayers to be in accord with God's will; and we want to express our commitment to doing God's will in our lives.

We can utter the phrase: "Thy will be done" with one of two attitudes. One is with a snarl: "Thy will be done." We resist. The other attitude is desire: "Thy will be done." Jesus himself epitomized the desire that God's will be done in Gethsemane, when he was on the edge of life: "not my will but yours be done" (Luke 22:42). God's will would be expressed in Christ's will to die for the sins of the world (1 John 2:2).

Forsyth wrote that "we can offer God nothing so great and effective as our obedient acceptance of the mind and purpose and work of Christ." Our will is to do God's will—as expressed in Jesus, who himself accepted God's will and carried out God's purpose through his work of dying for our sins.

---

19. P. T. Forsyth, *The Soul of Prayer* (London: Charles H. Kelly, 1916), 17. [2002 ed.—15.]

In our prayers, we desire and pray for God's will to be done. We accept "the mind and purpose and work of Christ," aligning ourselves with Jesus and what he said and did. Our attitude in prayer is obedient acceptance of God's will in Christ as we know God's will through Jesus himself.

This acceptance in obedience is not easy. But Forsyth notes that "it is a power that grows by exercise. At first it groans, at last it glides." As we daily seek God's will and obediently accept God's will, we find that we grow in grace with our wills more fully attuned and aligned with God's will.

May God grant us the grace to pray: "Thy will be done."

62

Final Forgiveness in Christ

> He is Christ and Lord by His cross. Christian faith is our life-experiences of complete and final forgiveness in Christ. It does not *include* forgiveness; it *is* forgiveness. Its centre is the centre of forgiveness. Only the redeemed Church, the Church that knows the forgiveness, has the key to the Saviour. His blessings are the key to His nature; they do not wait till the nature is first defined.[20]

FORSYTH ALWAYS ARGUED THAT we know who Jesus is by what Jesus did. In his cross, Christ is our savior. Through his death we become a "new creation" (2 Cor 5:17). Put technically, theologically, "the Christology turns on a Soter[i]ology" (25). For "the centre of Christ is where the centre of our salvation is. He is Christ, He is God, to us in that He saves us. And He is God by that in Him which saves us. He is Christ and Lord by His cross." God was in Christ, reconciling the world. This was what God was doing in the cross: "Christ was God reconciling" (27).

This meant for Forsyth that "Christian faith is our life-experiences of complete and final forgiveness in Christ. It does not *include* forgiveness; it *is* forgiveness. Its centre is the centre of forgiveness." Forgiveness, experienced in Christ, is the center and nature of our Christian life. This is the message we hear and experience: "Father, forgive them" (Luke 23:34). And we are forgiven,

---

20. P. T. Forsyth, *The Cruciality of the Cross* (London: Hodder and Stoughton, 1909), 25–26.

in Jesus Christ. Our forgiveness is "complete and final forgiveness" in Christ. Salvation is grounded in God's action in Jesus Christ and his cross. This is where faith begins and ends, with the work of Christ the savior.

The church knows this forgiveness. The "key to the savior" is forgiveness, experienced by faith and focused on God's redeeming, holy love in the cross of Jesus Christ. We know who Jesus is by what he has done. For Christ's "blessings are the key to His nature." The greatest blessing we can receive is this word of complete and final forgiveness: You are forgiven!

63

Christ Intercedes for Us

> The intercession of Christ is simply the prolonged energy of His redeeming work. The soul of Atonement is prayer. The standing relation of Christ to God is prayer. The perpetual energy of His Spirit is prayer. It is prayer (and His prayer) that releases for us the opportunities and the powers of the spiritual world.[21]

WHEN WE THINK OF the great work of Christ for us and our salvation, we think of his incarnation, his atonement, and his resurrection. But Christ's work does not stop there! A work of Christ that continues for us, always is his intercession. Paul wrote: "Who is to condemn? It is Christ Jesus, who died, yes, who was raised, who is at the right hand of God, who indeed intercedes for us" (Rom 8:34; cf. Heb 7:25). With every breath we take, Jesus Christ is interceding for us, "at the right hand of God." Imagine!

Christ advocates for us, interceding with God on our behalf. Forsyth said that "the intercession of Christ is simply the prolonged energy of His redeeming work. The soul of Atonement is prayer. The standing relation of Christ to God is prayer. The perpetual energy of His Spirit is prayer. It is prayer (and His prayer) that releases for us the opportunities and the powers of the spiritual world." Christ continues his work through his prayers for us—as

---

21. P. T. Forsyth, *God the Holy Father* (London: Independent, 1957), 94–95. Originally in *The Holy Father and the Living Christ* (1897).

through his death, his ongoing relation to God, and through the continuing energy of His Spirit.

Christ's prayer, says Forsyth, "releases for us the opportunities and the powers of the spiritual world." Think of that in relation to all our ministries and our service. Christ is interceding to enable us to have opportunities to be in communion with God and serve as Christ's disciples. His prayers give us the power to live out our faith in the ministries God gives us. Christ provides the opportunities and power for us to serve him—through his intercessory prayers. With our every breath, Christ is interceding for us . . . !

64
Ministry of the Word

> The strict successor of the Apostle is the New Testament, as containing the precipitate of their standard preaching. It is not the ministry that is the successor of the Apostolate, but the ministry *plus* the true apostolic legacy of the Bible—the ministry of *the Word*. The ministry is the successor of the Apostles only as the prolongation of their Bible—as the nervous system spreads the brain. The ministry of the Word is, therefore, not a projection or creation of the Church.[22]

DURING THE PROTESTANT REFORMATION, the issue of authority was central. Roman Catholics viewed the church as the primary authority since the church established the canon of Scripture, which books became the Holy Bible. This was the church's authority. The Protestant view was that the Scripture was the primary authority over the church. For the Scriptures were the record of the preaching and teachings of the apostles and of God's Word throughout history. The ministry of the Word was the church's proclamation of Scripture as God's Word. This has primary authority

Forsyth describes the issue above. The ministry of the church today is the successor to the apostles inasmuch as the ministry is based on the New Testament, which is "the precipitate" of the preaching of the apostles. This is the true "ministry of the Word."

---

22. P. T. Forsyth, *The Church and the Sacraments*, 3rd ed. (London: Independent, 1949 [1917]), 137.

The church's ministry is the successor to the apostles' ministry as it continues and extends the Bible—"as the nervous system spreads the brain," said Forsyth. The Word of God has priority over the church since it directly conveys what the apostles taught prior to the full establishment of the Christian church. The church is built on the Word (Eph 2:20).

Insofar as ministry today is grounded in the Scriptures and emerges from the biblical teachings of the apostles, it is a true ministry of the Word. For "the authority of the ministry is not drawn from the Church—only its opportunity is" (137–38). It is for us to be faithful to the witness of the apostles and to minister in the name of Jesus Christ, today.

65

The Kingdom in the Making

> History is no mere preparation for the Kingdom, it is the Kingdom in the making. The actual world is not only the workshop of God. It is His building in process. Therefore the Church has a world policy . . . a world passion and a world ideal.[23]

WE PRAY IN THE Lord's Prayer: "thy kingdom come, thy will be done" (see Matt 6:10). We look forward to when the reign of God comes in all its fullness. We look around us—in our culture and history—and we realize the fullness of God's reign has not yet come!

Yet, we may be lulled into thinking our current history—and what has gone before us and makes us who we are, today—that history, itself is simply "window dressing." We may think history itself does not matter since God's real and full kingdom will come sometime in the future.

But Forsyth cautions that "history is no mere preparation for the Kingdom, it is the Kingdom in the making. The actual world is not only the workshop of God. It is His building in process. Therefore the Church has a world policy, . . . a world passion and a world ideal."

History matters. What we do in history, matters. God is at work in history. God's purposes are being carried out in history.

23. P. T. Forsyth, *The Church and the Sacraments*, 3rd ed. (London: Independent, 1949 [1917]), 126.

We are part of God's purposes. The church is in history to serve God. The church has "a world passion and a world ideal." We are called by God to be disciples of Jesus Christ who minister to the world in his name. So we care about the world . . . and its people. God builds toward God's final reign—God's kingdom; and God builds in history and through history. God builds in us and through us. History matters in the fullest way! History is where we live on behalf of Jesus Christ. We do look forward to the final consummation of history: when the Lord will "reign forever and ever" (Exod. 15:18). But on our way to the future, we serve God in the slice of history we have been given!

66

The Counterpart of Christ

> God's end in Christ is a Church community. . . . It is the Church and not the individual that is the counterpart of Christ. If we are complete in Christ, we are complete only in a holy and Catholic Church.[24]

SOME CHRISTIANS BELIEVE THEY can be Christians all by themselves. They have a "private faith"—just themselves and God. They fit the definition of a "lone ranger" as someone who acts alone, not consulting or seeking to interact with others.

But this is not the Christianity of the New Testament. Jesus called a group of disciples. As the Christian message spread, "churches" grew up. Churches drew together all those who acknowledged Jesus Christ as their Lord and savior. Churches were eminently "social." Basic to the church was the apostle's command: "Be subject to one another out of reverence for Christ" (Eph 5:21).

Forsyth noted that "God's end in Christ is a Church community." For "it is the Church and not the individual that is the counterpart of Christ. If we are complete in Christ, we are complete only in a holy and Catholic Church."

As Christians, we are part of the "body of Christ" (1 Cor 12:27). Christ established a church community. This "people of God" (Heb 4:9) are disciples of Jesus Christ who live in fellowship and participation with one another. There is no "solitary"

---

24. P. T. Forsyth, *Christian Perfection* (London: Hodder & Stoughton, 1899), 17–18.

Christianity. There is no "lone ranger" Christianity. Our faith is eminently social. We join with other believers in devotion to be a "holy" people—those set apart for God's purposes and to do God's will.

So, said Forsyth, "If we are complete in Christ, we are complete only in a holy and Catholic Church. The fullness of our relationship with Christ comes only as we live holy lives, according to God's will; and as we share in the life of the "catholic church"—the church throughout the world, the universal people or "household" of God in Christ.

Let us commit ourselves to living more fully in the Christian community—the church. Let us celebrate the church as "the counterpart of Christ!"

67

Prayer Is Asking and Action

> Prayer is the powerful appropriation of power, of divine power. It is therefore creative. Prayer is not mere wishing. It is asking—with a will. Our will goes into it. It is energy. *Orare est laborare* [To pray is to work]. We turn to an active Giver; therefore we go into action.[25]

SOMETIMES OUR PRAYERS CAN seem like a passive activity. We pray, we speak from our hearts to God. Our petitions are our requests, our wishes. We believe God hears and answers our prayers.

But much more is happening in our prayers than we realize. We speak; God listens. God speaks; and we listen. In prayer we are laying hold of God's willingness to hear and answer us. God can help; and God will help.

But we have to work in prayer, too. Prayer calls for our active engagement. We put our energies into prayer because we believe God will be active in our prayers. As Forsyth put it: "Prayer is the powerful appropriation of power, of divine power. It is therefore creative. Prayer is not mere wishing. It is asking—with a will. Our will goes into it. It is energy. *Orare est laborare*. We turn to an active Giver; therefore we go into action."

"To pray is to work," said Forsyth. Do we work at our prayers? Or, do we cast our words into the air, casually? As we believe God

---

25. P. T. Forsyth, *The Soul of Prayer* (London: Charles H. Kelly, 1916), 11–12. [2002 ed.—11]

hears and answers, so we also must be energetic and persistent in following up on our prayers—hearing what God tells us to do; how to act to be able to receive God's answers in due time. We must contemplate the implications for our prayers. If we pray to be reconciled with someone, we must take steps to help make that reconciliation possible. Forsyth said "what we ask for chiefly is the power to ask more and to ask better." We ask "better" in prayer when we actively engage in following where our prayers lead us; and what they lead us to do. Prayer is asking . . . and action!

68

Trusting What Christ Did

> Our chief danger to-day is not the ceremonial ritual, but the moral and social ritual. It is the idea that men are to be saved by well-doing, by integrity, by purity, by generosity, by philanthropy, by doing as Christ did rather than trusting what Christ did, by loving instead of trusting love.[26]

FORSYTH'S EMPHASIS ON THE cross of Christ as the means of salvation and reconciliation of God with humanity reflects the emphasis of the New Testament: "But God proves his love for us in that while we still were sinners Christ died for us" (Rom 5:8).

The emphasis is on what God has done in Jesus Christ—doing for us what we cannot do for ourselves—attaining forgiveness of sin and transforming us into a "new creation" (Gal 6:15).

Like sixteenth-century Protestant theologians, Forsyth saw a danger in the belief that salvation comes by human efforts, by "good works," rather than by faith in what Jesus Christ has done in dying for us. For, "by grace you have been saved through faith, and this is not your own doing; it is the gift of God—not the result of works, so that no one may boast" (Eph 2:8–9). Forsyth wrote: "Our chief danger to-day is not the ceremonial ritual, but the moral and social ritual. It is the idea that men are to be saved by well-doing, by integrity, by purity, by generosity, by philanthropy, by doing as

---

26. P. T. Forsyth, *Christian Perfection* (London: Hodder & Stoughton, 1899), 87-88.

Christ did rather than trusting what Christ did, by loving instead of trusting love." Again: "We are not saved by the love we exercise, but by the Love we trust" (71).

All forms of "virtue" or pride in one's achievements—however noble or significant they may be—can turn us away from the gospel truth towards the mistaken notion that salvation is by human action, rather than by the action of Jesus Christ through his death on the cross. The impulses Forsyth mentions—well-doing, integrity, purity, generosity—are temptations to trust these self-achievements, rather than trusting what Christ did. We, however, trust God's love in Christ, not our own actions—even in loving!

69

Become What We Are and Are Not

> We have to work out into practice what we are in principle, to become what we are and are not, to fight sins because we are freed from sin. And failures in practice, however dangerous, are not the same as the great failure to place ourselves on the side of righteousness and holiness all our days.[27]

THEOLOGICALLY, "SANCTIFICATION" IS OUR growth in holiness and in faith. After we have been "justified by faith" (Rom 3:28)—received the gift of salvation—we live out our faith by the work of the Holy Spirit within us (1 Pet 1:2). We fight against and resist sin (2 Cor 7:1), which is no longer the reigning power within us. Now we are "dead to sin and alive to God in Christ Jesus" (Rom 6:11). We live by faith and grow in grace. Forsyth writes that "we have to work out into practice what we are in principle, to become what we are and are not, to fight sins because we are freed from sin."

But Christians still sin and we fail to follow the Spirit and to do what God desires. Our Christian lives are a continual repentance. We sin and need forgiveness. We experience "the sin that clings so closely" (Heb 12:1).

But we should not lose heart in our Christian lives. God forgives our sin through Jesus Christ and God's Holy Spirit does not leave us or forsake us (Heb 13:5). The bigger perspective is the

---

27. P. T. Forsyth, *Christian Perfection* (London: Hodder & Stoughton, 1899), 46.

work of God, even as sin still occurs. We have a "zig-zag" Christian experience. Forsyth indicates that "failures in practice, however dangerous, are not the same as the great failure to place ourselves on the side of righteousness and holiness all our days." Our life is "hidden with Christ in God" (Col 3:3). This is the great story of our lives. This is who we truly are, our primary identity. Our constant task is to "become what we are"—with the "Spirit bearing witness with our spirit that we are children of God" (Rom 8:16). We become what we are; and resist "what we are not."

70
God's Desire Is Communion with Us

> Perfection is not sinlessness. The "perfect" in the New Testament are certainly not the sinless. And God, though He wills that we be perfect, has not appointed sinlessness as His object with us in this world. His object is communion with us through faith.[28]

OUR CHRISTIAN LIVES SHOULD not be marked by fear of not "being perfect" in the sense of no longer sinning. We are realistic to know that even as Christians we still sin. We need daily forgiveness; and know "sinlessness" will never be achieved in this life. As Forsyth wrote, "Perfection is not sinlessness. The 'perfect' in the New Testament are certainly not the sinless. And God, though He wills that we be perfect, has not appointed sinlessness as His object with us in this world."

Instead, God has another, important purpose. For God's "object is communion with us through faith," said Forsyth. God desires communion with us. This is the communion that comes through faith. It is expressed in prayer and in ways we serve God in this world as an expression of faith. Forsyth notes: "We need God for Himself. He Himself is the end. We need chiefly communion with Him; which is not confined to the perfectly holy but is open to all in faith, and possible along with cleaving [separating from] sin" (12–13). Our communion or fellowship with God through faith is

---

28. P. T. Forsyth, *Christian Perfection* (London: Hodder & Stoughton, 1899), 11–12.

what God desires and what we need. Our relationship with God through faith is ours as a gift by the Holy Spirit, moving us to seeking God's will in all we do. We want to obey God's will and follow God's way. We desire to have a mature, more complete faith, made possible by our hearts loving God above all else. Forsyth said God "does not offer us communion to make us holy." But God "makes us holy for the sake of communion." As our faith grows, our communion with God becomes stronger. We are drawn deeper into the life of God. "Christian perfection is the faith which justifies, puts you right with God," said Forsyth (84). God desires communion with us, through faith!

71

Forgiveness of Old Life and New

> Faith is not the faith of the sinless but of the redeemed, not of the holy but of the sanctified, the faith and the love of those who have been forgiven much, forgiven often and long, forgiven always. The very nature of faith is trust of a Saviour, who is not the saviour of my past but of my soul; and it is trust for forgiveness, for forgiveness not only of the old life but of the new.[29]

THOSE WHO KNOW JESUS Christ know him as our savior from sin. Our offenses against the holy God; our following our own ways in life instead of God's ways; our attitudes and actions against others—all these—and more!—constitute our sin, for which we need divine forgiveness.

God sent Jesus Christ to be our savior: "For our sake he made him to be sin who knew no sin, so that in him we might become the righteousness of God" (2 Cor 5:21). Christ brings forgiveness which we accept by faith. Faith is the means by which our redemption is received. Through faith, forgiveness becomes real. Forsyth wrote that "faith is not the faith of the sinless but of the redeemed, not of the holy but of the sanctified, the faith and the love of those who have been forgiven much, forgiven often and long, forgiven always."

---

29. P. T. Forsyth, *Christian Perfection* (London: Hodder & Stoughton, 1899), 7.

Faith's "very nature" is "trust of a Saviour," said Forsyth. We trust Jesus Christ who brings the forgiveness we could never obtain by ourselves or bring to ourselves. Christ is our savior. He is "not the saviour of my past but of my soul; and it is trust for forgiveness, for forgiveness not only of the old life but of the new."

God in Christ forgives the sins of our past. They are forgiven, forgotten, forever by God. But we also trust Christ's forgiving power continuing for us in the present—day by day; and into the future. Christ brings forgiveness in our new life, forever!

72

A New Heart

> Salvation, if it means anything real, means a new heart; and the new heart is not simply a new affection, but a new relation, a new man, the conscience forgiven, recreated, and reassured before God by the atoning, reconciling act of God. That is real religion, real faith.[30]

WE ARE SAVED BY Christ's death on the cross for our salvation (1 Thess 5:9–10). Christ's death provides the atonement for our sin, reconciliation with God (Rom 5:10–11), and forgiveness (Acts 10:43). Forsyth stressed that "without atonement there is no justice done to the moral order." The holy God acts to provide a way of salvation for sinners. Salvation comes by the work of the Holy Spirit, not by our own conscience or power—"but by God's Spirit in the conscience" (64). Salvation is God's work within us.

What emerges within us—by faith—is a complete new life! Forsyth wrote that "salvation, if it means anything real, means a new heart; and the new heart is not simply a new affection, but a new relation, a new man [person], the conscience forgiven, recreated, and reassured before God by the atoning, reconciling act of God. That is real religion, real faith."

The heart is the center of our affections. To receive a new heart, by God's Spirit, is to have our complete selves—including all our affections—now to belong to God in Christ. Our new heart

---

30. P. T. Forsyth, *Missions in State and Church: Sermons and Addresses* (London: Hodder & Stoughton, 1908), 65.

is our new relationship with God. We become a "new creation" (2 Cor 5:17), so it is "no longer I who live, but it is Christ who lives in me" (Gal 2:20). Our sin is forgiven. Our lives are "recreated." We are assured of our forgiveness through the atoning act of Jesus Christ who reconciled us with God. This is "real faith," Forsyth said. We have a "conversion of the conscience by the Holy Spirit." The prophetic promise is fulfilled in Christ: "A new heart I will give you, and a new spirit I will put within you" (Ezek 36:26).

73
All the Accounts Are Kept

> The non-intervention of God bears very heavy interest, and He is greatly to be feared when He does nothing. He moves in long orbits, out of sight and sound. But He always arrives. Nothing can arrest the judgment of the Cross, nothing shake the judgment-seat of Christ. The world gets a long time to pay, but all the accounts are kept—to the uttermost farthing. Lest if anything were forgotten there might be something unforgiven, unredeemed, and unholy still.[31]

WE LIVE OUR LIVES, day by day, one day at a time. We think of what is coming next week or next month. We seldom think beyond our immediate calendars.

But what of history ahead? What of divine judgment? What of the reckoning of all past history in the actions of God in relation to all people ... and to us?

Forsyth declares all this is coming. God may appear to be doing "nothing," moving "in long orbits, out of sight and sound." God may not appear to be on the scene. But God "always arrives," said Forsyth. For "nothing can arrest the judgment of the Cross, nothing shake the judgment-seat of Christ." The judgment of Christ's cross stands over history ... and over all us. This is sure and certain.

While we live, day by day, "the world gets a long time to pay," said Forsyth. We may not think about it. But "all the accounts

---

31. P. T. Forsyth, *The Justification of God* (New York: Charles Scribner's Sons, 1917), 216.

are kept—to the uttermost farthing." God's moral will permeates history. Through the many centuries, God's work continues. The warning is all too real: "for you reap whatever you sow" (Gal 6:7): "All the accounts are kept."

God is at work to redeem and sanctify all things in heaven and earth. As all the accounts are kept, so, the judgment of Christ will take place, "lest if anything were forgotten there might be something unforgiven, unredeemed, and unholy still."

74

Concrete Prayer

> It is somewhat fruitless to ask for a general grace to help specific flaws, sins, trials, and griefs. Let prayer be concrete, actual, a direct product of life's real experiences. Pray as your actual self, not as some fancied saint. Let it be closely relevant to your real situation. Pray without ceasing in this sense. Pray without a break between your prayer and your life. Pray so that there is a real continuity between your prayer and your whole actual life.[32]

SOMETIMES WE CAN LAPSE into "general prayers," like "God bless everybody!" These may have a place. Forsyth would call them prayers for "general grace" like general prayers "to help specific flaws, sins, trials, and griefs." But he did not believe these were very fruitful.

Instead: pray specifically. Pray concretely. Sometimes this advice has been called ESP—Experiment in Specific Prayer. As Forsyth put it, "Let prayer be concrete, actual, a direct product of life's real experiences. Pray as your actual self, not as some fancied saint. Let it be closely relevant to your real situation." We can be specific in our prayers to God. We can pray about things we care most about in life, our actual life experiences. We can be brutally honest in our prayers. We can pray as our "actual self," not—as Forsyth put it: "as some fancied saint." Our honesty and openness

---

32. P. T. Forsyth, *The Soul of Prayer* (London: Charles H. Kelly, 1916), 95. [2002 ed.—74.]

before God mark the vitality of our communion with our Lord. Our prayers should reflect our real-life cares and concerns.

In this, we can "pray without ceasing" (1 Thess. 5:17). We can pray "without a break between your prayer and your life. Pray so that there is a real continuity between your prayer and your whole actual life." If we commend our real-life cares and anxieties to God, we communicate what is deep within us to God in prayer. We will share our realities with God as we reflect upon them. This is the continuity between our life and our prayers.

We should practice ECP: Experiment in Concrete Prayer!

75
Our Chief Certainty

> What we become more sure of than anything else is that God has done what makes Him surer of us than we are either of ourselves or of Him. Our chief certainty is God's certainty of us in Christ. And our religious knowledge is not to know God but to know that we are known of Him.[33]

WHAT IS YOUR CHIEF certainty in life? What are you more convinced of and confident in than all else?

These questions point us back to our most basic realities. When we take away all that surrounds us—what is left? What is our chief certainty?

Forsyth maintained we can come to a point where "what we become more sure of than anything else is that God has done what makes Him surer of us than we are either of ourselves or of Him." Imagine, we are more sure of God than we are of ourselves or of our belief in God! Have you reached that point?

Forsyth continued to name our greatest certainty: "Our chief certainty is God's certainty of us in Christ. And our religious knowledge is not to know God but to know that we are known of Him." In Jesus Christ, we experience our highest certainty: that we are known by God. God sent Jesus Christ to die for us; to forgive and reconcile us. In Jesus Christ we have our greatest certainty. In

---

33. P. T. Forsyth, *The Principle of Authority in Relation to Certainty, Sanctity and Society* (London: Independent, 1913; 2nd ed. 1952), 35.

him, we see God's holy love in action. This is the greatest knowledge we can attain; and the most comforting and secure knowledge we can be given.

God knows us in Jesus Christ! This is true faith. This is the knowledge we need for life in communion with God. To be known by God in Christ means we can give ourselves away in God's service, secure in the certain knowledge that nothing in "all creation, will be able to separate us from the love of God in Christ Jesus our Lord" (Rom 8:39).

76

Faith Is Obedience

> Faith does not simply involve submission; it *is* submission. The obedience of faith is not an obedience that flows from faith; it is faith as obedience.... Faith is nothing except as an obedience.[34]

WE OFTEN THINK OF "faith" in various ways. Faith is what we believe. Faith is how we live. Faith is what he hope for and wish we "have."

Forsyth put it very clearly. Faith is submission. Faith is submission to the will of God. This is the relinquishing of our own wills to the greater will of God. This is our constant posture. It is what we desire most of all. Our prayer will always be that of Jesus: "not my will but yours be done" (Luke 22:42).

This means simply that faith is *obedience*. Said Forsyth: "The obedience of faith is not an obedience that flows from faith; it is faith as obedience." To submit to God's will in Christ is to obey God's will in Christ. Faith is to act on our inner submission and follow where God leads. We are disciples of Jesus Christ who, as with Jesus' first disciples, "got up and followed him" (Mark 2:14).

Faith as obedience leads our lives into many directions. There are times we act in faith which leads us into situations and acts of obedience we would not have imagined or contemplated. Faith as obedience can put us at risk. Faith as obedience can lead us into

---

34. P. T. Forsyth, *The Principle of Authority in Relation to Certainty, Sanctity and Society* (London: Independent, 1913; 2nd ed. 1952), 324.

forms of ministry we could not have envisioned. The inner compulsion of faith makes these actions necessary for us. We cannot not act in faithful obedience to the will of God in Jesus Christ as we come to know it by the work of the Holy Spirit in our lives.

"Faith is in its nature an obedience . . . obedience always" (12). We obey, in trust, believing God is with us. God calls us to follow no matter what the destination, what the cost, or what the actions God calls us to take may be.

77

God Is for Us

> He is our God, not because He loved and pitied, but because in His love and pity He redeemed us. God is for us and our release only that we may be for Him and His service. He is for us, to help, save and bless, only that we may be for Him, to worship Him in the communion of the Spirit and serve Him in the majesty of His purpose for ever. First we glorify Him, then we enjoy Him for ever.[35]

THEOLOGIANS HAVE DECLARED GOD'S "being" is expressed in God's "actions." Who God *is* becomes known to us in what God *does*.

Forsyth combined God's "being" and God's "actions" when he wrote that God is our God "not because He loved and pitied, but because in His love and pity He redeemed us." God redeemed us from sin in the cross of Jesus Christ, the Son of God. In this: "God proves his love for us in that while we still were sinners Christ died for us" (Rom 5:8). Jesus Christ is God's love in action.

In Jesus Christ we see God is "for us." Christ is our redeemer. Christ saves us, releasing us from sin, so we can live for Christ and for God's purposes. Forsyth wrote that "God is for us and our release only that we may be for Him and His service." God is "for us, to help, save and bless, only that we may be for Him, to worship Him in the communion of the Spirit and serve Him in the majesty

---

35. P. T. Forsyth, *The Principle of Authority in Relation to Certainty, Sanctity and Society* (London: Independent, 1913; 2nd ed. 1952), 13.

of His purpose for ever." God is "for us" so we can be "for God." We worship God, live in communion with God through the Holy Spirit, and serve God and live for God's purposes, now and forever.

Forsyth hearkens to the Westminster Shorter Catechism (1647) when he said, "First we glorify Him, then we enjoy Him for ever." God is "for us": God redeems us and we serve God!

78
Faith as Personal Trust

> Faith is the soul's answer to his grace, it is not the heart's answer to love. It is nothing else than personal trust in the personal God in Christ, the personal response to, and appropriation of, God's own personal and eternal act of pardoning and redeeming grace in Christ.[36]

GOD'S GRACE, SAID FORSYTH, is "religious pardon" (124), a "personal reconciliation with God" (125). Grace is "not a gift to life"—just added to us; but "the gift of life" itself (125). Grace is "entirely bound up with the person and work of Christ as the power of God unto salvation."

"Faith" is "the soul's answer to his grace, it is not the heart's answer to love. It is nothing else than personal trust in the personal God in Christ, the personal response to, and appropriation of, God's own personal and eternal act of pardoning and redeeming grace in Christ."

Faith is real when we realize we are trusting God, the same God who has reconciled us through Jesus Christ and given us new life, as a divine gift. We trust God in a personal way, entrusting ourselves to God for the whole of our lives. We receive God's eternal act of pardoning our sin on the basis of Christ's death on the cross; and receiving grace, which makes our whole life and

---

36. P. T. Forsyth, "The Church's One Foundation," *London Quarterly Review* (October 1906) in Marvin W. Anderson, ed., *The Gospel and Authority: A P. T. Forsyth Reader* (Minneapolis: Augsburg, 1971), 125.

existence new—to be lived in freedom and obedience to the God who has redeemed and saved us in Christ Jesus.

Faith cannot be received from anyone other than God—through the work of the Holy Spirit. Faith must be personally appropriated. We cannot live on the faith of our parents or friends, or anyone else. Faith receives God's act of pardoning our sins in Christ. Faith receives reconciliation with God, the new relationship of trust and love for God which orients our lives.

God's grace brings us faith. We receive the gift of salvation and reconciliation as we personally trust our savior.

79
Sacraments as the Word Visible

> The Word and the Sacraments are the two great expressions of the Gospel in worship. The Sacraments are the acted Word-variants of the preached Word. They are signs, but they are more than signs. They are the Word, the Gospel itself, visible, as in preaching the Word is audible. But in either case it is an act. It is Christ in a real presence giving us anew His Redemption. . . . It means an act in which he intends to convey *Himself*, His mind, His will, His act.[37]

A GREAT FOCUS OF Protestantism in worship is on the Word and the Sacraments. They are the two great expressions of the gospel of Jesus Christ.

Forsyth called the sacraments (Baptism and the Lord's Supper) "the acted Word-variants of the preached Word." Sacraments "act out" the Word of God in Scripture. "They are," said Forsyth, "signs, but they are *more* than signs." Some Protestants have said sacraments are *only* "signs," a pointer or a remembrance. But Forsyth maintained sacraments are "the Word, the Gospel itself, visible, as in preaching the Word is audible." Sacraments are the visible words of God. Sacraments do not merely "bring to mind" a truth, they actually communicate Christ and the message of the gospel itself. Sacraments are acts by which God's grace in Jesus Christ comes to us.

37. P. T. Forsyth, *The Church and the Sacraments*, 3rd ed. (London: Independent, 1949 [1917]), 176.

In the sacraments, we have "Christ in a real presence giving us anew His Redemption." The sacraments convey Jesus Christ to us and give us the benefits of his work of salvation. Or, we can say, the sacraments "represent" Christ but they also "present" Christ—through them we receive the benefits and blessings of what Christ has done in redemption, for us! Said Forsyth, a sacrament "means an act" in which Jesus Christ "intends to convey *Himself*, His mind, His will, His act." In the sacraments—before our eyes!—we see what Jesus Christ has done in his life, death, and resurrection to bring us salvation and new life!

80

Relation to God over Behavior

> The error at the root of all false ideas of perfection is this: it is rating our behaviour before God higher than our relation to God—putting conduct before faith, deeds before trust, work before worship.[38]

OUR BEHAVIOR—OUR ACTIONS IN life are important. Those outside the Christian faith "find their own ways" with how they live. They choose paths and directions, perhaps based on some convictions about reality; or some forms of moral standards. Their emphasis may be on trying to live up to their ideals, which they believe can bring fulfillment.

In Christian faith, our behavior matters too. We show the genuineness of our Christian faith by how we live our lives. Actions reflect beliefs. Christians live in obedience to God's will and purposes—known in the law of God—while looking to Jesus Christ as our model for the ways God wants us to live. Because we are "in Christ" (Rom 6:11), we believe what matters most is "faith working through love" (Gal 5:6).

Yet Christians need to keep the right focus, too. Forsyth wrote that "the error at the root of all false ideas of perfection is this: it is rating our behavior before God higher than our relation to God—putting conduct before faith, deeds before trust, work before worship." We can never look at our acts of love, or faith,

---

38. P. T. Forsyth, *Christian Perfection* (London: Hodder & Stoughton, 1899), 68.

and begin to find in them actions that somehow make us "perfect" or righteous before God. Our deeds, behavior, and actions *express* our faith; they do not *cause* or create our faith.

Our faith is focused on Jesus Christ and our relationship with him. Our union with Christ by faith is the vital heartbeat of Christian faith. Our relation with God in Christ is what's most important, what matters most. *Faith* is our means of salvation; not our actions or what we do.

81

Church Is New Creation of God in the Holy Spirit

> It is a new creation of God in the Holy Spirit, a spiritual organism, in which we find our soul. Men unite themselves with the Church because already united with Christ, and because they are, in that very act of union with Him, already in spirit and principle organised into the great Church He created, and whose life He is.[39]

We can look at the Christian church in various ways. First, we may think of the church building. It is the visible expression of "church" and one with which people are most familiar.

But for members of the church, there is so much more! We experience the church as a fellowship of those who confess faith in Jesus Christ (1 Cor 1:9). The church is the "body of Christ" (1 Cor 12:27); it is the "communion of saints," as the Apostles' Creed says.

These expressions of the church by its members point us to what Forsyth said when he wrote the church is "a new creation of God in the Holy Spirit, a spiritual organism, in which we find our soul." We are part of the church by God's work in giving us faith in Jesus Christ by the power of the Holy Spirit. In Christ—in the church, we "find our soul." We worship our creator, redeemer, and sustainer: God the Father, Son, and Holy Spirit!

---

39. P. T. Forsyth, *The Church and the Sacraments*, 1st ed. (London: Independent, 1917), 34.

Forsyth went on to say that people "unite themselves with the Church because already united with Christ, and because they are, in that very act of union with Him, already in spirit and principle organised into the great Church He created, and whose life He is." We are part of the church before we may even realize it! When we are united with Christ by faith, we are already part of Christ's church. We are grafted into Christ, and we are joined together with all other believers in the body of Christ, the church. We draw our life and mission from the great "head of the church" (Eph 5:23), Jesus Christ, our Lord and savior! Praise God for the church as the new creation of God!

82

Adjusting the Compass

> The Church must always adjust its compass at the Cross.[40]

THE CHRISTIAN CHURCH IS active in many ways. When you look at a local congregation, you'll find many different "programs," activities, "missions" or things that regularly take place in the church's life. Church members express their faith and callings in the church's various ministries.

How does the church know what to do? The New Testament does not give a specific "blueprint" for how believers today—over twenty centuries later—should carry out their missions as the "body of Christ" (1 Cor 12:27), those who together love and serve Jesus Christ by following Christ's words and deeds, by expressing their faith by what they do in service to God and to others in the world! As Jesus said, "Those who love me will keep my word" (John 14:15). So how is the church to get its orientation and direction?

Forsyth offered succinct advice: "The Church must always adjust its compass at the Cross." The cross of Jesus Christ is where atonement for "the central human situation—the situation of sin and guilt" was made (52). We receive the revelation of the atonement for our sins by faith. For those who believe, this reality

---

40. P. T. Forsyth, Article III in Fréderic Louis Godet, ed., *The Atonement in Modern Religious Thought: A Theological Symposium*, 3rd ed. (London: James. Clarke, 1907), 52. Rpt. *God of Holy Love: Essays of Peter Taylor Forsyth*, ed. and intro., Paul K. Moser and Benjamin Nasmith (Eugene, OR: Pickwick, 2019), 28.

shapes lives and life directions as they live out their redemption and forgiveness of sins (Col 1:14).

So also for the church. What the church does in its mission and ministry in the world must witness to the atoning death of Christ on the cross. What Christ's death means—for the world and individuals—must be expressed by the church in what it believes and what it does. The church must always call people to faith in Christ. It must also live out meanings of Christ's death as it serves the world in obedience to Jesus Christ himself who said to his disciples: "I am among you as one who serves" (Luke 22:27).

The church constantly adjusts its "compass" to point toward ministries of service and love that witness to the crucified Christ who gave his life for the sin of the world (John 1:29).

83

The Condensation of History

> Christ is the condensation of history.[41]

WE WONDER ABOUT HUMAN history—how will it all end; and also our own history—where do our lives find their meaning and purpose? These are big questions and ones that are important to us.

Forsyth provided a helpful sentence: "Christ is the condensation of history." Forsyth was speaking of what Christ did—in his death on the cross as an atonement for sin—"his victorious death" and also his "risen life," which have "power to unite the race to himself, and to work his complete holiness into its actual experience and history."

This insight is very meaningful for us. It means that in Jesus Christ we find the meaning for all history; and the meaning of our lives themselves. Christ's reconciliation covers "the whole of history" and enters into each of us by the Spirit. The cross sets up "a new covenant and a new humanity in which Christ dwells as the new righteousness of God." Believers are united with Christ in his resurrection and Jesus Christ is "the eternal guarantee of the historical consummation of all things some great day."

The end of history is secured: Christ is victorious! History's ultimate meaning is the meaning Jesus Christ gives to history—and to those united with him—every day. The meaning for our lives is found in living in the "new covenant" as the "new humanity" as

---

41. P. T. Forsyth, *The Work of Christ* (London: Hodder & Stoughton, 1910), 130.

Christ lives in us by the power of the Holy Spirit. "Christ is the condensation of history" means that as we live in a "living union" with Christ—following his will and his way for our lives—we find our ultimate meaning and purpose for our lives. We are redeemed by Jesus Christ in his cross—sin forgiven and reconciled with God—to be God's "new humanity" in Christ in the world, as we serve others through Jesus Christ. We live and serve as we await the consummation of history itself—now assured to us in Christ's "victorious death and risen life."

84

All Is Well

> There are those who can quietly say, as their faith follows their love into the unseen, "I know that land beyond. Some of my people live there. Some have gone abroad on secret service there, which does not admit of communications. But I meet from time to time the commanding officer—the one in charge both here and there—and when I mention them to Him, He assures me all is well."[42]

IN THE APOSTLES' CREED, we confess we believe in "the life everlasting." And so we do.

We do not know details of the future life. We have great images of the saints in everlasting glory, forever praising God: "Hallelujah! For the Lord our God the Almighty reigns. Let us rejoice and exult and give him the glory" (Rev 19:7).

We also confess in the Creed our belief in the "resurrection of the body." The nature of our resurrection bodies is also unknown. But our assurance is that eternal life in the presence of God, in heaven, is beyond our imaginings and the God who is with us in life is also with us in death and throughout eternity.

Forsyth's poignant passage above witnesses to this faith. Our relationships in this life are valued and transformed, taking on eternal significance. Our assurance in faith is that in the death and

---

42. P. T. Forsyth, *This Life and the Next: The Effect on This Life of Faith in Another* (New York: Macmillan, 1918), 44.

resurrection of Jesus Christ, we are joined, eternally, with God and with each other.

For P. T. Forsyth, the last word, in life and in death, is: "All is well." We live by this faith, established by God's holy love expressed in Jesus Christ who gives us eternal life, even as we anticipate our eternal fellowship and praise in the presence of God, forever. All belongs and exists for God, including us!

All is well!

Sources Cited

Anderson, Marvin W., ed. *The Gospel and Authority: A P. T. Forsyth Reader.* Minneapolis: Augsburg, 1981.

Forsyth, P. T. "Article III" in Fréderic Louis Godet, ed., *The Atonement in Modern Religious Thought: A Theological Symposium.* 3rd ed. London: James. Clarke, 1907.

———. *Christian Perfection.* London: Hodder & Stoughton, 1899.

———. *The Church and the Sacraments.* 1st ed. London: Independent, 1917.

———. *The Church and the Sacraments.* 3rd ed. London: Independent, 1949.

———. "The Church's One Foundation." *London Quarterly Review* 106 (October, 1906) 193–202.

———. *The Cruciality of the Cross.* London: Hodder & Stoughton, 1909.

———. *Faith, Freedom, and the Future.* London: Hodder & Stoughton, 1912.

———. *God the Holy Father.* London: Independent, 1957.

———. *The Justification of God: Lectures for War-Time on a Christian Theodicy.* New York: Charles Scribner's Sons, 1917.

———. "The Need for a Positive Gospel." *London Quarterly Review* 101 (January 1904) 64–99.

———. *The Person and Place of Jesus Christ.* London: Hodder & Stoughton, 1909.

———. *Positive Preaching and Modern Mind.* The Lyman Beecher Lectures on Preaching, Yale University. London: Hodder & Stoughton, 1907. Reprint of 2nd ed. in *P. T. Forsyth: The Man, The Preachers' Theologian, Prophet for the 20th Century.* Pittsburgh: The Pickwick Press, 1981. 3rd ed. published as *Positive Preaching and the Modern Mind.* London: Independent, 1949.

———. *The Principle of Authority in Relation to Certainty, Sanctity and Society.* London: Independent, 1913 (2nd ed. 1952).

———. "Religion and Reality." *The Contemporary Review* 115 (May 1919) 548–54.

———. "Revelation and the Bible." *Hibbert Journal* 10 (October, 1911) 235–52.

———. *Revelation Old and New: Sermons and Addresses.* Edited by John Huxtable. London: Independent, 1962.

———. *Rome, Reform and Reaction: Four Lectures on the Religious Situation.* London: Hodder & Stoughton, 1899.

———. *The Soul of Prayer.* London: Charles H. Kelly, 1916. Reprint, Vancouver, BC: Regent College Publishing, 2002.

———. *This Life and the Next: The Effect on This Life of Faith in Another.* New York: Macmillan, 1918,

———. *The Work of Christ.* London: Hodder & Stoughton, 1910.

Moser, Paul K., and Benjamin Nasmith, ed. *God of Holy Love: Essays of Peter Taylor Forsyth.* Eugene, OR: Pickwick, 2021.

Selected Resources for Further Reflection

Benedetto, Robert. *P. T. Forsyth Bibliography and Index*. Bibliographies and Indexes in Religious Studies, Number 27. Westport, CT: Greenwood, 1993.

Bradley, William L. *P. T. Forsyth: The Man and His Work*. London: Independent, 1952.

Brown, Robert McAfee. *P. T. Forsyth: Prophet for Today*. Philadelphia: Westminster, 1952.

———. "P. T. Forsyth." In *A Handbook of Christian Theologians*, edited by Martin E. Marty and Dean G. Peerman, 144–65. Cleveland, OH: World, 1965.

Goroncy, Jason. *Descending on Humanity and Intervening in History: Notes from the Pulpit Ministry of P. T. Forsyth*. Eugene, OR: Pickwick, 2013.

———. *Hallowed Be Thy Name: The Sanctification of All in the Soteriology of P. T. Forsyth*. T. & T. Clark Studies in Systematic Theology. London: Bloomsbury T. & T. Clark, 2013.

Hart, Trevor, ed. *Justice the True and Only Mercy: Essays on the Life and Theology of Peter Taylor Forsyth*. Edinburgh: T. & T. Clark, 1995.

Hunter, A. M. *P. T. Forsyth*. Philadelphia: Westminster, 1974.

Leow, Theng Huat. *The Theodicy of Peter Taylor Forsyth: A "Crucial" Justification of the Ways of God to Man*. Eugene, OR: Pickwick, 2011.

McKim, Donald K. "The Authority of Scripture in P. T. Forsyth." Pittsburgh Theological Seminary, 1973. The Library, Presbyterian Theological Seminary, Richmond, Virginia.

———, ed. *Encyclopedia of the Reformed Faith*. Louisville, KY: Westminster/John Knox, 1992.

Mikolaski, Samuel J., ed. *The Creative Theology of P. T. Forsyth: Selections from His Works*. Grand Rapids: Eerdmans, 1969.

———. "P. T. Forsyth." In *Creative Minds in Contemporary Theology*, edited by Philip Edgcumbe Hughes, 306–39. Grand Rapid: Eerdmans, 1969.

Miller, Donald G., Browne Barr, and Robert S. Paul. *P. T. Forsyth: The Man, The Preachers' Theologian, Prophet for the 20th Century*, including a reprint of P. T. Forsyth, *Positive Preaching and the Modern Mind*. The Pittsburgh Theological Monograph Series, Number 36. Pittsburgh: Pickwick, 1981.

Rodgers, John H. *The Theology of P. T. Forsyth: The Cross of Christ and the Revelation of God*. London: Independent, 1965.

Rogers, Jack B., and Donald K. McKim. *The Authority and Interpretation of the Bible: An Historical Approach.* San Francisco: Harper & Row, 1979.

Sell, Alan P. F. *Nonconformist Theology in the Twentieth Century: The Didsbury Lectures 2006.* Milton Keynes, UK: Paternoster, 2006.

———, ed. *P. T. Forsyth: Prophet for a New Millennium?* London: United Reformed Church, 2000.

Worrall, B. G. "The Doctrine of Authority in the Theology of P. T. Forsyth." PhD diss., Durham University. Available at Durham E-Theses Online: http://etheses.dur.ac.uk/9768/.

Electronic Resources

Jason Goroncy, "Some P. T. Forsyth Resources": https://jasongoroncy.com/category/pt-forsyth/.
Paul K. Moser, "P. T. Forsyth": https://pmoser.sites.luc.edu/ptforsytharchive/
P. T. Forsyth texts online: https://archive.org/search.php?query=peter%20taylor%20forsyth/.
P. T. Forsyth texts on Google Books: https://www.google.com/search?tbm=bks&q=%22peter+taylor+Forsyth%22/.

Printed in Great Britain
by Amazon